SCHOLASTIC

100 LITERACY FRAMEWORK LESSONS

TERMS AND CONDITIONS

IMPORTANT - PERMITTED USE AND WARNINGS - READ CAREFULLY BEFORE USING

Minimum specification:
- PC with a CD-ROM drive and 512 Mb RAM (recommended)
- Windows 98SE or above/Mac OSX.1 or above
- Recommended minimum processor speed: 1 GHz

YEAR 6

Scottish Primary 7

Nikki Hughes, Roger Hurn & Gill Matthews

CREDITS

Authors
Nikki Hughes, Roger Hurn
& Gill Matthews
Additional material for
revision section written
by Nikki Gamble

Commissioning Editor
Fiona Tomlinson

Development Editor
Simret Brar

Project Editor
Rachel Mackinnon

Editor
Linda Mellor

Series Designer
Joy Monkhouse &
Anna Oliwa

Designers
Anna Oliwa,
Andrea Lewis,
Catherine Perera & Geraldine Reidy

Book Designer
Q2A Media

Illustrations
Theresa Tibbetts, Christophe
Berthould & Robin Edmonds /
Beehive Illustration

CD-ROM Development
CD-ROM developed in association
with Vivid Interactive

Narrative © 2007, Nikki Hughes
Non-fiction © 2007, Gill Matthews
Poetry © 2007, Roger Hurn
Revision © 2007, Scholastic Ltd
© 2007 Scholastic Ltd

Designed using Adobe InDesign

Published by Scholastic Ltd
Villiers House
Clarendon Avenue
Leamington Spa
Warwickshire CV32 5PR
Visit our website at
www.scholastic.co.uk

Printed by Bell and Bain Ltd
1 2 3 4 5 6 7 8 9   7 8 9 0 1 2 3 4 5 6

ACKNOWLEDGEMENTS

The publishers gratefully acknowledge permission to reproduce the following copyright material: **Gerry Bailey** for the use of 'Chips get the chop' by Gerry Bailey © 2007, Gerry Bailey © 2007, Gerry Bailey (2007, previously unpublished); for the use of 'Healthy school dinners' by Gerry Bailey © 2007, Gerry Bailey (2007, previously unpublished); for the use of 'The Invasion' by Gerry Bailey © 2007, Gerry Bailey (2007, previously unpublished) and for the use of 'Creatures of the Deep' by Gerry Bailey © 2007, Gerry Bailey (2007, previously unpublished). **Laura Cecil Literary Agency** on behalf of The James Reeves Estate for the use of 'The sea' by James Reeves from *Complete poems for children* by James Reeves © 1998, James Reeves (1998, Classic Mammoth). **Pie Corbett** for the use of 'City Jungle' by Pie Corbett from *Rice, Pie and Moses* by John Rice, Pie Corbett and Brian Moses © 1995, Pie Corbett (1995, Macmillan Children's Books). **Coregeo Limited** for the use of 'Stop the rot' from the website www.sundownerapples.co.uk/juicyscience © Coregeo Limited. **The Cornish and Devon Post Series** for the use of an extract from an article 'After the freeze come the floods' from *The Cornish and Devon Post* 9th February 1963 © 1963, The Cornish and Devon Post series. **Vince Cross** for the use of 'Hajj' by Vince Cross © 2007, Vince Cross (2007, previously unpublished). **John Foster** for the use of 'Haikus' by John Foster from *The Works* chosen by Paul Cookson © 2000, John Foster (2000, Macmillan Children's Books). **A.M. Heath and Co. Ltd** for the use of an extract from *Pig-Heart Boy* by Malorie Blackman © 1997, Malorie Blackman (1997, Doubleday). **David Higham Associates** for the use of an extract from *Kensuke's Kingdom* by Michael Morpurgo © 1999, Michael Morpurgo (1999, Heinemann Young Books) and for the use of extracts from 'Into the Dark' by Henrietta Branford from *Centuries of Stories* edited by Wending Cooling © 1999, Henrietta Branford (1999, Collins). **Roger Hurn** for the use of 'The Storm', 'The Dancing Bear', 'My Mum' and 'The Land of Tir Na Nog' all by Roger Hurn © 2007, Roger Hurn (2007, previously unpublished). **Lion Hudson plc** for the use of 'Mum' by Andrew Fusek Peters and Polly Peters from *Mad, bad and dangerously haddock* by Andrew Fusek Peters © 2006, Andrew Fusek Peters and Polly Peters (2006, Lion Hudson plc). **Michaela Morgan** for the use of 'Blake's Tyger - Revisited' by Michaela Morgan from *Through a window: Literature and Culture* selected by Wendy Body © 1995, Michaela Morgan (1995, Longman). **The Maggie Noach Literary Agency** as representative of the author for the use of an extract from 'The Valley of Crocuses' by Jean Ure, first published in *Centuries of stories* edited by Wendy Cooling © 1999, Jean Ure (1999, HarperCollins Limited). **Campbell Perry** for the use of 'From frogspawn to frogs born' by Campbell Perry © 2007, Campbell Perry (2007, previously unpublished); for the use of 'Letter of complaint' by Campbell Perry © 2007, Campbell Perry (2007, previously unpublished) and for the use of 'Making mountains' by Campbell Perry © 2007, Campbell Perry (2007, previously unpublished). **The Random House Group Ltd** for the use of text from *Beyond the Deepwoods: The Edge Chronicles* by Paul Stewart and Chris Riddell Text and illustration © 1998, Paul Stewart and Chris Riddell (1998, Doubleday). **Scholastic Children's Books** for the use of an extract from *My Story: Battle of Britain – Harry Woods England 1939–1941* by Chris Priestley © 2002, Chris Priestley (2002, Scholastic Children's Books) and for the use of an extract from *A darkling plain* by Philip Reeve © 2006, Philip Reeve (2006, Scholastic Children's Books). **Short Books** for the use of an extract from *Who was Charlotte Bronte?* by Kate Hubbard © 2004, Kate Hubbard (2004, Short Books). **Walker Books Limited** for the use of an extract from *The Falcon's Malteser* by Anthony Horowitz © 1986; 1995, Anthony Horowitz (1986; 1995, Walker Books Ltd) and for the use of an extract and illustration from *Extreme animals: the toughest creatures on earth* by Nicola Davies, illustrated by Neal Layton. Text © 2006, Nicola Davies; illustration © 2006, Neal Layton (2006, Walker Books Limited London SE11 5HJ) **Celia Warren** for the use of 'Jersey lizard' by Celia Warren © 2007, Celia Warren (2007, previously unpublished). **Chris Webster** for the use of 'Mars', 'Global warming fears' and 'Internet dangers and delights' all by Chris Webster from *All new 100 Literacy hours: Year 6* by Chris Webster © 2006, Chris Webster (2006, Scholastic Limited).

Every effort has been made to trace copyright holders for the works reproduced in this book, and the publishers apologise for any inadvertent omissions.

British Library Cataloguing-in-Publication Data
A catalogue record for this book is available from the British Library.
ISBN 978-0439-94526-4

CONTENTS

INTRODUCTION
100 Literacy Framework Lessons: Year 6

About the series

The *100 Literacy Framework Lessons* series is a response to the Primary National Strategy's revised Literacy Framework and contains **all new** material. The lessons mirror the structure and learning objectives of the Exemplification Units of the Framework. The CD-ROM provides appropriate and exciting texts and also contains a variety of other resources from videos and images to audio and weblinks, which will help to guide you in implementing the Framework's emphasis on ICT texts. The books and CD-ROMs will be an invaluable resource to help you understand and implement the revised Framework.

The key points of the revised framework are:

- The development of early reading and phonics;
- Coherent and progressive teaching of word-level and sentence-level embedded into learning or taught discretely;
- Following and building upon the teaching sequence from reading to writing and developing comprehension;
- Flexible lessons providing a challenging pace;
- Integration of speaking and listening skills;
- Planning for inclusion;
- Broadening and strengthening pedagogy.

Early reading and phonics

The authors of the *100 Literacy Framework Lessons* have endeavoured to incorporate all of the above with one exception, the teaching of phonics. The Government is advising that phonics is taught using a systematic, discrete and time-limited programme. However, where possible we have made links to phonic focuses that you might want to identify when teaching the lesson.

It is important to note that the renewed Framework is advocating a change from the Searchlight model of teaching early reading to the 'simple view of reading', "*The knowledge and skills within the four Searchlight strategies are subsumed within the two dimensions of word recognition and language comprehension of the 'two simple views of reading'. For beginner readers, priority should be given to securing word recognition, knowledge and skills*" (from the PNS Core Papers document). Phonic work will be time limited and as children develop their early reading skills they will then move from learning to read to learning to learn.

Boscastle flood photo 1

Using the book

The book is divided into three parts, called Blocks: Narrative Block, Non-fiction Block and Poetry Block. This reflects the structure of the renewed Framework planning. The Blocks are divided into Units, each Unit covers a different text-type within the Block, for example in the Narrative Block there might be one Unit which covers 'myths and legends' and another that covers 'plays'. Units are taught on a specified amount of weeks and are split into Phases. Phases vary in length and are essentially a way to focus on a specific part of teaching relating to the Unit. Phases are then divided into days, or lessons, which then contain the teaching activities. Unlike the *100 All New Literacy Hours,* this book has not been divided into terms because one of the main points of the Framework is flexibility and this structure will let teachers adapt to their particular children's needs.

Block [genres] ➤ Units [text-type] ➤ Phases [section of Unit] ➤ Days/Lessons [Individual lessons]

Units

Each Unit covers a different text-type, or genre and because of this each Unit has its own introduction containing the following:

Objectives: All objectives for the Unit are listed under their strand names.

Progression: Statements about the progression that the children should make within the Unit's focus, for example narrative text-type.

Aspects of learning: Key aspects of learning that the Unit covers.

Prior learning: Key elements that the children need to be able to do before they commence the lessons.

Cross-curricular opportunities: Integrating other areas of the curriculum into the literacy lessons.

Resources: Everything required for the lesson that teachers may not have readily available.

Teaching sequence: This is an overview chart of the Unit. It shows the number of Phases, children's objectives, a summary of activities and the learning outcomes.

Unit lesson plans

The lesson plans all follow the same format. There are three columns and each contains different information.

Key features: The key features column provides an at-a-glance view of the key aspects of learning covered in the lesson.

Stages: The stages column provides the main lesson plans.

Additional opportunities: This column provides additional opportunities for the lesson. This is where there will be links made to phonics, high frequency words, support or extension activities and any other relevant learning opportunities.

End of Phase

At the end of each Phase there are three boxes containing Guided reading or writing ideas, Assessment ideas and Further work.

Guided: The guided box contains ideas for guided reading or writing. These have been included separately as there seems to be a trend to do this work outside of the literacy hour lesson. These ideas can either be integrated into a lesson or taught at a separate time.

Assessment: There are two types of assessment.

End of Phase assessments: These are mainly observations of the children or simple tasks to see whether they have understood what has been taught in the Phase. Teachers are referred back to the learning outcomes in the teaching sequence in the Unit introduction.

End of Unit assessments: These are activities which range from interactive activities, to working from a stimulus image, to completing a photocopiable sheet. They can be found on the CD-ROM accompanying this series.

Further work: Further work provides opportunities for the teacher to extend or support the children following the assessment activity.

Photocopiable pages

At the end of each Unit are the photocopiable pages. These can also be found on the CD-ROM.

Using the CD-ROM

This is a basic guide for using the CD-ROM; for more detailed information please go to 'How to use the CD-ROM' on the start-up screen of the CD-ROM.

The CD-ROM contains resources for each book in the series. These might include: text extracts, differentiated text extracts, editable text extracts, photocopiable pages, interactive activities, images, videos, audio files, PowerPoint files, weblinks and assessment activities. There are also skeleton frames based on Sue Palmer's skeletons for teaching non-fiction text types. Also on the CD-ROM are the lesson notes for easy planning as Word file documents.

   You can access resources in a number of ways:

Phase menu: The Phase menu provides all the resources used in that Phase. There are tabs at the top of the page denoting the resource type, for example 'Text'. If you click on this tab you will see a series of buttons to your left; if you press these then you will be taken to the other texts used within that Phase. You can print two versions of the text: either the screen – which shows any annotations made (see Whiteboard tools below) or Print PDF version, which will print an A4 size.

Resources menu: The resource menu lists every resource that is available on the CD-ROM. You can search by type of resource.

Whiteboard tools: This series contains a set of whiteboard tools. These can be used with any interactive whiteboard and from a computer connected to a projector. The tools available are: Hand tool – so that when you zoom in you can move around the screen; Zoom in; Zoom out; Pen tool for freehand writing or drawing; Highlighter; Line tool; Box tool; Text tool; Eraser tool; Clear screen; Hide annotations; Colour. You cannot save any changes made to the texts so always remember to 'Print Screen' when you annotate the CD-ROM pages.

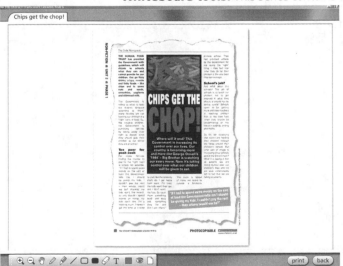

Speak and listen for a ange of purposes on paper and on screen strand checklist	Narrative Unit 1	Narrative Unit 2	Narrative Unit 3	Narrative Unit 4	Non-fiction Unit 1	Non-fiction Unit 2	Non-fiction Unit 3	Non-fiction Unit 4	Poetry Unit 1	Poetry Unit 2
Strand 1 Speaking										
Use a range of oral techniques to present persuasive arguments and engaging narratives.			✔	✔		✔	✔		✔	✔
Participate in whole-class debate using the conventions and language of debate, including Standard English.							✔			✔
Use techniques of dialogic talk to explore ideas, topics or issues.	✔	✔	✔		✔	✔		✔	✔	✔
Strand 2 Listening and responding										
Make notes when listening for a sustained period and discuss how note taking varies depending on context and purpose.				✔	✔	✔				
Analyse and evaluate how speakers present points effectively through use of language and gesture.							✔		✔	✔
Listen for language variation in formal and informal contexts.							✔			
Identify the way spoken language varies according to the differences in context and purpose of use.							✔	✔		✔
Strand 3 Group discussion and interaction										
Consider examples of conflict and resolution, exploring language used.										
Understand and use a variety of ways to criticise constructively and respond to criticism.	✔		✔					✔	✔	✔
Strand 4 Drama										
Improvise using a range of drama strategies and conventions to explore themes such as hopes, fears, desires.		✔	✔			✔				✔
Consider the overall impact of a live or recorded performance, identify dramatic ways of conveying characters' ideas and building tension.									✔	
Devise a performance considering how to adapt the performance for a specific audience.					✔					✔

Read for a range of purposes on paper and on screen strand checklist

	Narrative Unit 1	Narrative Unit 2	Narrative Unit 3	Narrative Unit 4	Non-fiction Unit 1	Non-fiction Unit 2	Non-fiction Unit 3	Non-fiction Unit 4	Poetry Unit 1	Poetry Unit 2
Strand 5 Word recognition										
Objectives covered by the end of Year 2.										
Strand 6 Word structure and spelling										
Spell familiar words correctly and employ a range of strategies to spell difficult and unfamiliar words.			✔		✔	✔				
Use a range of appropriate strategies to edit, proofread and correct spelling in own work, on paper and on screen.	✔	✔	✔	✔	✔	✔	✔	✔	✔	✔
Strand 7 Understanding and interpreting texts										
Appraise a text quickly, deciding on its value/quality/usefulness.					✔	✔				
Understand underlying themes, causes and points of view.	✔			✔	✔				✔	✔
Understand how writers use different structures to create coherence and impact.	✔	✔		✔				✔	✔	✔
Explore how word meanings change when used in different contexts.										
Recognise rhetorical devices used to argue, persuade, mislead and sway the reader.						✔	✔			
Strand 8 Engaging with and responding to texts										
Read extensively and discuss personal reading with others, including in reading groups.			✔						✔	✔
Sustain engagement with longer texts, using different techniques to make the text come alive.		✔	✔		✔	✔				
Compare how writers from different times and places present experiences and use language.	✔	✔			✔	✔	✔	✔	✔	✔

Write for a range of purposes on paper and on screen strand checklist

	Narrative Unit 1	Narrative Unit 2	Narrative Unit 3	Narrative Unit 4	Non-fiction Unit 1	Non-fiction Unit 2	Non-fiction Unit 3	Non-fiction Unit 4	Poetry Unit 1	Poetry Unit 2
Strand 9 Creating and shaping texts										
Set own challenges to extend achievement and experience in writing.		✔	✔		✔		✔			
Use different narrative techniques to engage and entertain the reader.	✔	✔	✔	✔	✔	✔				
In non-narrative, establish, balance and maintain viewpoints.						✔				
Select words and language drawing on their knowledge of literary features and formal and informal writing.	✔	✔			✔	✔		✔	✔	✔
Integrate words, images and sounds imaginatively for different purposes.		✔		✔	✔	✔		✔		
Strand 10 Text structure and organisation										
Use varied structures to shape and organise text coherently.	✔	✔	✔	✔	✔	✔	✔	✔	✔	✔
Use paragraphs to achieve pace and emphasis.	✔		✔		✔		✔			
Strand 11 Sentence structure and punctuation										
Express subtle distinctions of meaning including hypothesis, speculation, supposition, by constructing sentences in varied ways.	✔	✔	✔		✔	✔		✔		
Use punctuation to clarify meaning in complex sentences.	✔	✔	✔				✔	✔		
Strand 12 Presentation										
Use different styles of handwriting for different purposes with a range of media, developing a consistent and personal legible style.	✔	✔	✔				✔		✔	✔
Select from a wide range of ICT programs to present text effectively and communicate information and ideas.		✔	✔		✔	✔		✔	✔	

NARRATIVE
UNIT 1 Fiction genres

Speak and listen for a range of purposes on paper and on screen

Strand 1 Speaking
- Use the techniques of dialogic talk to explore ideas, topics or issues.

Strand 3 Group discussion and interaction
- Understand and use a variety of ways to criticise constructively and respond to criticism.

Read for a range of purposes on paper and on screen

Strand 6 Word structure and spelling
- Use a range of appropriate strategies to edit, proofread and correct spelling in own work, on paper and on screen.

Strand 7 Understanding and interpreting texts
- Understand underlying themes, causes and points of view.
- Understand how writers use different structures to create coherence and impact.

Strand 8 Engaging with and responding to texts
- Compare how writers from different times and places present experiences and use language.

Write for a range of purposes on paper and on screen

Strand 9 Creating and shaping texts
- Use different narrative techniques to engage and entertain the reader.
- Select words and language drawing on their knowledge of literary features and formal and informal writing.

Strand 10 Text structure and organisation
- Use varied structures to shape and organise texts coherently.
- Use paragraphs to achieve pace and emphasis.

Strand 11 Sentence structure and punctuation
- Express subtle distinctions of meaning, including hypothesis, speculation and supposition, by constructing sentences in varied ways.
- Use punctuation to clarify meaning in complex sentences.

Strand 12 Presentation
- Use different styles of handwriting for different purposes with a range of media, developing a consistent and personal legible style.

Progression in narrative

In this year children are moving towards:
- Identifying story structures typical to particular fiction genres; recognising that narrative structure can be adapted and events revealed in different ways (such as stories within stories, flashbacks, revelations); analysing the paragraph structure in different types of story and noting how links are made; making judgements in response to story endings (for example whether it was believable, whether dilemmas were resolved satisfactorily).
- Identifying stock characters in particular genres and looking for evidence of characters that challenge stereotypes and surprise the reader, such as in parody; recognising that authors can use dialogue at certain points in a story to (for example) *explain plot, show character and relationships, convey mood or create humour.*

▶

UNIT 1 ◄ Fiction genres *continued*

Key aspects of learning covered in this Unit

Information processing
Children will identify and refine classification criteria and sort fiction examples accordingly. They will quickly appraise particular texts and look for a range of information clues to support classification of texts into different genres.

Evaluation
Children will share responses and outcomes orally and in writing. They will apply the criteria they have identified in order to make decisions and judgements. They will give feedback to others and judge the effectiveness of their own work.

Reasoning
Children will construct reasoned arguments based on their views and responses to the books or stories read.

Empathy
In discussing and writing about the books or stories, children will need to imagine themselves in another person's position. They will explore techniques that facilitate this process.

Communication
Children will develop their ability to discuss and debate issues and personal responses in respect of both the form and the content of the stories they are reading and writing. They will often work collaboratively in pairs and groups. They will communicate outcomes orally and in writing.

Prior learning

Before starting this Unit check that the children can:
■ Identify and discuss the various features of a fiction text; including the structure and organisation and the way language is used to create effects.
■ Discuss their responses to a range of fiction they have read.
■ Use a range of approaches and learning strategies, to extend and explore their understanding of and response to works of fiction.
If they need further support please refer to a prior Unit or a similar Unit in Year 5.

Resources

Phase 1:
A collection of fiction books of a range of different genres; *Creatures of the deep Extracts 1, 2* and *3* by Gerry Bailey ✿; *The Falcon's Malteser* by Anthony Horowitz ✿; *Beyond the Deepwoods* by Paul Stuart and Chris Riddell ✿; *Into the dark Extracts 1* and *2* by Henrietta Branford ✿; Photocopiable page 24 'Genre features'

Phase 2:
The Valley of the Crocuses by Jane Ure from *Centuries of Stories* edited by Wendy Cooling (Collins); *The Valley of the Crocuses* ✿; Photocopiable page 25 'Story ladder'; *Into the dark Extracts 1* and *2* by Henrietta Branford ✿; *The Invasion Extracts 1* and *2* by Gerry Bailey ✿; *Email from Stuart Blake* by Nikki Hughes ✿

Phase 3:
Pictures of potential story settings for a variety of genres; Photocopiable page 26 'Describe a setting'; Story cards ✿; Photocopiable page 25 'Story ladder'; Props for story telling; Assessment activity 'Identifying genre'

Cross-curricular opportunities

History – Invaders and settlers, Ancient Greece, Ancient Egypt, Victorians

UNIT 1 ■ Teaching sequence

Phase	Children's objectives	Summary of activities	Learning outcomes
1	I can identify a range of fiction genre and discuss which ones I prefer.	Classify books according to genre. Highlight features of a range of genre. Discuss reading preferences. Give a presentation on one genre.	Children can identify the features of a range of children's fiction genres. Children can discuss their preferences.
2	I can analyse the structure and language features of a short story.	Analyse story structure. Text marking for language and organisational features.	Children can identify the structure and language features of a short story.
3	I can plan, draft and write a short story in a genre of my choice.	Generate description of a story setting using a visual prompt. Generate a character portrait using a visual prompt. Plan a short story. Write a short story. Evaluate a short story. Retell a short story orally.	Children can plan, draft and write a short story using the features of their chosen genre.

Provide copies of the objectives for the children.

DAY 1 ▪ Exploring fiction genres

Key features	Stages	Additional opportunities
	### Introduction Organise the children into pairs as talk partners. Ask them to discuss with their partner which fiction genres they have read or know about and which genres they enjoy reading. Ask them to think of titles of books from these genres. Take answers from the children and generate a class list of different fiction genres – historical, mystery, crime, ghost, funny and so on. Ask the children to work with their talk partner again and discuss whether they can name any features of these genres such as character types, settings, plots, themes. Discuss their answers and begin class *Features of...* lists for the genres previously listed. Display the lists in the classroom.	**Support:** organise into groups according to their reading ability, and collections of books assigned accordingly
Information processing: identify classification criteria and sort fiction examples	### Independent work Organise the children into small groups of four or five. Give each group a collection of fiction books from the class library to classify into groups according to genre. Those needing support could be given the name of the fiction genres contained in their collection. Those needing an extension activity could be given paper to write down the features of the different genres they have identified in their collection.	**Extend:** select their own titles from the class library/carry out a 'genre hunt' from a given list of genres **Support:** investigate the work of one author
	### Plenary Ask each group to feed back to the class on their classification. Ask them to state the genres they found, the titles in each category and any features they know relating to those genres. Are there certain authors who always write a particular genre? Make class lists of some of the titles for each genre on large paper to be displayed on the wall.	

DAY 2 ▪ Exploring science fiction and mystery

Key features	Stages	Additional opportunities
Information processing: identify and refine classification criteria	### Introduction Display *Creatures of the deep* extracts from the CD-ROM. Read them to the class. Ask the children which fiction genre they think it is (science fiction) and ask them to pick out evidence to support their views. Model identifying the features of science fiction by annotating text; for example, typical characters such as aliens, typical plot – invasion of Earth, use of language features which create suspense. Display *The Falcon's Malteser* extract from the CD-ROM. As above, read and identify the features of the mystery genre – clues to solving the mystery contained in the text, familiar characters/settings, detective. Add features found in the two extracts to the class *Features of...* lists. Ask the children to share which extract they preferred and give reasons why. Establish that we all have different reading preferences.	**Support:** differentiate the text types according to ability range **Extend:** persuade each other why one text type is better than another
	### Independent work Give the children other short extracts from mystery and science fiction books to read independently. Ask them to identify the genre and annotate the texts (highlighting/underlining/labelling), picking out features of the genre using the *Features of...* checklists created by the class. Decide which story they would want to read and why, prepare reasons.	
	### Plenary Discuss together the children's preferences. Ask them which extracts they preferred, and why. Is it because of the plot, the setting or something else?	

DAY 3 ■ Exploring fantasy and historical genre

Key features	Stages	Additional opportunities
	Introduction Read *Beyond the Deepwoods*, a fantasy story, and *Into the deep* Extracts 1 and 2. Establish the settings, characters, plot. Model identifying the features of each genre by annotating the texts (from checklists devised with children) and add any further features to the lists. Refer to photocopiable page 24 'Genre features'. Discuss the reading preferences of the children.	
Information processing: sort fiction examples	**Independent work** Select further extracts from the fantasy and historical genres for the children to read independently. Annotate texts with features of the genre (from the checklist). Decide which story they would want to read and why; prepare reasons. Texts selected can be differentiated according to reading ability. Less confident readers may need to work with adult support.	**Support:** give children a frame to complete such as setting, character, plot **Extend:** hold a debate where children are given one of the genres to defend
Communication: personal responses	**Plenary** In pairs, children should talk to their partner about which genre they preferred from the four read to them, and why. Ask children to feedback to the class the preferences and reasons of their partner.	

DAY 4 ■ Genre presentations – preparation

Key features	Stages	Additional opportunities
	Introduction Tell the children they are going to be working on a presentation about a genre of their choice. Discuss the intended audience for the presentation (children of their own age). Show them the following subheadings (this could be presented as a contents page): ■ Features of the genre ■ Authors and titles ■ Why I enjoy reading this genre ■ Recommended books ■ Extract(s) On the board, model planning a presentation based on one genre, such as fantasy. Discuss what could be included under each heading. Organise the children into pairs according to their preferred genre and mixed-ability, if appropriate.	**Support:** some children may have limited experience of a range of genre; they could be given a particular genre and titles/authors to research
Communication: work collaboratively in pairs	**Independent work** Ask the children to work in their pairs to plan a presentation about the chosen genre. Give choices of presentation – oral presentation, mind map, poster, ICT presentation. Put together a range of titles from the different genres available in the classroom.	**ICT:** presentations could include pictures, extracts, sound files
	Plenary Join pairs together to make groups of four. Ask each pair to tell the other about their chosen genre. Remind the children to use the subheadings from the introduction.	

DAY 5 ◾ Genre presentations

Key features	Stages	Additional opportunities
	Introduction Remind children of the content needed for their presentations by recapping on the subheadings. Discuss with the children what makes an effective presentation – clear information, well organised and so on. Together, create a *Making a presentation* checklist to use to assess the presentations (audible, looking at the audience, visual aids and so on).	
Communication: work collaboratively in pairs	**Independent work** Ask the children to continue working with their partners on their genre presentations, in their chosen format. They may wish to research their chosen genre beyond the titles they have read, they could either do this by searching for the genre on the internet or by being given suggestions from the teacher. When choosing an extract to include, ask them to try and choose one which reflects the features of the genre. Allow some time for children to rehearse their presentations.	
Evaluation: apply criteria to make judgements	**Plenary** Invite pairs present to the rest of the class. The class should provide feedback on the presentations, based on the checklist created together in the introduction. After listening to all of the presentations, ask children to record one or two titles they would like to read based on the recommendations. Display the presentations in the classroom or make them available in a book for reference.	**Extend:** before presenting, children can proofread their work to check for spelling, clarity, punctuation, omissions and so on

DAY 6 ◾ Using genre language features

Key features	Stages	Additional opportunities
	Introduction Give a bullet-pointed illustration of a simple incident, such as a journey home from school. For example: ■ Collect belongings and leave building. ■ Walk across playground. ■ Turn left onto pavement. ■ Stop at shop. ■ Leave shop, run home. Model writing an account of the incident using the language features of one of the genre studied.	
	Independent work Children should write accounts of the same incident in a range of different genres. Make checklists of features available (use photocopiable page 24 'Genre features'). Less confident writers could be provided with a writing frame and given fewer features to include in their writing.	**Support:** write a group account with adult scribing
Information processing: appraise different texts	**Plenary** Invite the children to swap accounts without revealing the genre they were writing in. They should each identify the genre of the piece they are reading and list the features used that enabled them to identify it. They could also feedback on any improvements that could be made to the text.	

Guided reading

Focus on a different genre with each guided reading group. Ask the group to feedback to the class on their genre and contribute to class display.

Further work

Create class recommendation lists by genre.
Complete book reviews and keep for reference, by genre.
Read an example of a parody and discuss features.
Work in small groups to write own parody, for example of a fairy tale.

DAY 1 ■ Historical fiction

Key features	Stages	Additional opportunities
	### Introduction You will need the full story *The Valley of the Crocuses* by Jan Ure from *Centuries of Stories* edited by Wendy Cooling or another short story in the historical genre. Before reading, tell children you will be asking them to look for clues as to the genre of the short story they are going to hear. Remind them of work done in Phase 1. Read the *Valley of the Crocuses* extract from the CD-ROM. While reading, ask children to identify the features of historical fiction contained within the text (historical references, names of characters, speech).	**Support:** provide children with the beginning of the diary entry (for example, from Caroc's point of view), or sentence starters for them to finish
Empathy: imagine themselves in another person's position	### Speaking and listening Stop at various points in the story and invite children to be hot-seated as the characters of Caroc, Fion, the parents and a villager. Ask them how they feel about the events; what do they think will happen in the future, what do they want to happen?	
	### Independent work Ask the children either to write a diary entry as one of the characters or a newspaper article reporting the fleeing of the village. You may need to recap on the features of this type of writing.	
	### Plenary Read the rest of the story. Ask the children questions about the story – was that how they expected it to end? How would the characters have felt?	

DAY 2 ■ Analysing story structure

Key features	Stages	Additional opportunities
	### Introduction As a class complete photocopiable page 25 'Story ladder', to show the structure of the story *The Valley of the Crocuses*: ■ Opening – setting and main character introduced ■ Build up – we are told of troubled times, Saxons invading ■ Problem – villagers have to flee village ■ Events – Caroc loses his dog, they hide in the forest (fast-forward to modern day) ■ Resolution – Caroc as an old man telling story of finding his dog ■ End – modern day dog finds a crocus in a hole. Note the handling of time – connectives, fast-forward, character's recollections.	
	### Independent work Give children an alternative short story in the same genre, for example *Into the Dark* from the CD-ROM. Ask them either to create a story ladder (photocopiable page 25) or a tension graph for this story.	**ICT:** use the downloadable 'Story Modeller' ITP (from Primary Strategy website) to construct a tension graph of the story
Communication: communicate outcomes orally	### Plenary Invite the children to share and explain their story ladders or tension graphs. Discuss differing interpretations.	**Extend:** ask more confident learners to create graphs for individual characters

DAY 3 ■ Features of historical fiction

Key features	Stages	Additional opportunities

Introduction

Display the list of features of historical fiction from Phase 1. With the children, text mark *The Valley of the Crocuses* extract highlighting the organisational and language features of the genre (set in the past, characters appropriate to time, old-fashioned language, based on fact).

Information processing: appraise particular texts

Independent work

Give children other extracts from *The Valley of the Crocuses* and *Into the dark* or other extracts from historical fiction. Ask them to text mark their extract in the same way. Make the checklist of features available. Less confident learners could be paired with a more confident child or could be given a simplified text and asked to identify fewer features, using a prepared table.

Plenary

Recap on complex sentences, model writing one or two sentences about one of the stories read. For example: *As the Saxons advanced on the village the women and children fled to the forest, leaving the men to fight.* Using individual whiteboards, ask the children to construct two or three complex sentences to summarise one of the stories they have read in this Unit.

Extend: write a short extract of their own using the features of the genre

Support: give clauses to arrange into complex sentences (fleeing from the village, the Saxons could be heard, grabbing his dog as he ran...)

DAY 4 ■ Science fiction

Key features	Stages	Additional opportunities

Introduction

Read *The Invasion Extract 1* from the CD-ROM, noting the build-up of tension in the story through the use of short sentences and clauses. Identify the author's use of punctuation in the text. Discuss who *they* might be, picking out the description of the creatures. Establish that the text is written in the science fiction genre and highlight the features shown in the text. Pause at the end of the extract.

Speaking and listening

Ask a child to volunteer to be hot-seated as the main character/narrator about how they feel, what they have seen, what they are going to do next, why and so on.

Empathy: imagine themselves in another person's position

Independent work

The narrator says: *It's ten days now since this began. Ten days of hell.* Ask the children to write a diary entry/entries describing what has happened during that time. Remind them to use the details in the text (for example, the rumbling sound, the flashes of colour) and to think about what might have happened to his family.

Communication: communicate outcomes orally

Plenary

Invite children to share their diary entries written as the character.

Extend: show the children the *Email from Stuart Blake* from the CD-ROM and ask them to write a response advising him what to do

DAY 5 ■ Analysing story structure

Key features	Stages	Additional opportunities

Introduction

Display *The Invasion Extract 2* from the CD-ROM. Model text marking the language features used: how tension is created, description, use of punctuation, character's feelings and so on. Look at the structure of both extracts – story opening creating tension and introducing *them*; build up, describing more about character's actions/creatures, flashback to the start of the holiday and so on. As a class, construct a tension graph to illustrate the structure of the story.

Information processing: appraise particular texts

Independent work

In pairs, text mark a different section of this or another science fiction text using the checklist for science fiction writing. Children should find examples of how the author creates tension, describes the creatures, the setting used, how the plot develops.

Support: text mark the same section read in the introduction independently

Plenary

Work through the text(s) annotated by the children, asking them to identify the features. They could share effective examples of tension being created, description of creatures and so on.

Guided reading

Read short stories from a range of genre, focusing on the features discussed in lessons.

Assessment

Can children describe the structure of a short story?
Can children create a tension graph for a short story?
Can children identify the language features used in a particular genre? Refer back to the learning outcomes on page 11.

Further work

Create a *How to spot a...* guide covering the range of genre.

DAY 1 ■ Describing a setting

Key features	Stages	Additional opportunities
	### Introduction	
	Look at pictures of story settings that could be used in a variety of genres, such as fantasy, ghostly, detective or historical. Choose one and model generating a description, using the detail in the picture. Ask the children to talk with response partners about what the place is like, what is happening there, who lives there and so on. Take ideas and together create a mind map describing the chosen setting. Model using effective adjectives, adverbs, similes and metaphors. Children should choose which setting they would like to use for their story.	
Communication: work collaboratively in groups	### Independent work	
	Organise the children into groups according to the setting they have chosen. Ask them to generate a description of their setting, organised as a mind map under headings – what it looks like, what you can hear, who lives there, what is happening. Encourage them to use effective vocabulary, adverbs, similes and so on.	**Display:** the settings pictures could be displayed while children read out their description for the class to guess which picture they are describing
	### Plenary	
	Put children into pairs with a child who looked at a different setting. Ask them to look at the pictures and the descriptions, share ideas, give feedback and comment on any gaps in the descriptions/questions that the reader might want answered.	

DAY 2 ■ Describing a setting (2)

Key features	Stages	Additional opportunities
	### Introduction	
	Choose one of the setting pictures. Ask the children who worked on this picture in Day 1 to share their ideas about what is happening there, what it is like, who lives there. Invite all the children to generate descriptions of this setting on their individual whiteboards; encourage effective vocabulary. Take the children's ideas and label the picture with good examples of description.	**Support:** begin by labelling the nouns in the picture, then adding an adjective for each noun, then a verb, then an adverb – building up their descriptive phrases
	### Independent work	
	Give the children photocopiable page 26 'Describing a setting' with the picture of their chosen setting in the middle and sections around the outside for writing their descriptive phrases. Encourage the use of effective vocabulary (adjectives, adverbs, powerful verbs), for example *luscious grass waving gracefully in the wind, the magnificent mountain dominating the sky...*	
Evaluation: judge the effectiveness of their own work	### Plenary	
	Children should assess their own work, highlighting the most effective phrase(s) used in their description. Ask them to share these with the class; you could make a list of the most descriptive phrases to display.	

DAY 3 ■ Character portraits

Key features	Stages	Additional opportunities
Communication: working collaboratively in pairs	### Introduction Display Story cards from the CD-ROM which show characters – boy, girl, wizard, alien creature, soldier and so on. Choose one character and as a class, discuss them. *Who are they? What do they do? Where do they live?* Ask the children to talk to a response partner and distribute the cards, one per pair. Encourage them to talk about their character's life, abilities, family, personality, ambitions and so on. Take ideas from some of the pairs.	
	### Independent work Invite children to choose a character they wish to develop in their story. This does not have to be the same one they discussed with a partner in the Introduction. At this point, children may wish to decide the genre they will be writing their short story in. Ask the children to create a character portrait. They could be provided with a writing frame or subheadings to explore about their character (as in the introduction).	**Support:** give children the picture of a character and ask them to write notes around the picture about them
Empathy: imagine themselves in another person's position	### Plenary As a class, create a list of interview questions to ask the characters. Pair the children to interview each other as their character, using the questions generated. This could be done as a whole class activity.	

DAY 4 ■ Planning a short story

Key features	Stages	Additional opportunities
	### Introduction Remind children of the generic story structure – opening, build up, problem, events, resolution, ending. Photocopiable page 25 'Story ladder' could be used as a planning frame. Model planning a story using one of the settings and one of the characters from the cards given; make explicit the genre it will be written in. Discuss possible openings of stories – action, speech, flashback. Discuss how the story needs a problem and how it could be resolved.	**Support:** plan a story as a group or be given the problem and they have to plan the other stages
	### Independent work Children should plan their own stories independently, using the same structure as modelled in the introduction (photocopiable page 25). Remind children to stick to the genre they have chosen, refer them to the features lists from earlier in the Unit.	
Evaluation: give feedback to others	### Plenary Ask the children to work with a 'critical friend' explaining the plan for their story. The critical friend's role is to ask questions and suggest improvements to the plan. (The children may need to develop a set of guidelines for how to work with a critical friend if they are not used to this.)	

DAY 5 ■ Short story writing – opening

Key features	Stages	Additional opportunities
	Introduction Model writing the start of the story from the plan written in Day 4. Discuss the intended audience for the story. Model using the language features of the genre and careful choice of vocabulary. Focus on sentence and paragraph construction, ensuring a combination of short and complex sentences. Model correct use of punctuation. Children could be included in the writing process by inviting them to write the next sentence or 'describe the...' on their individual whiteboards. Incorporate effective examples into the text.	**Support:** use a writing frame or paragraph starters to help them structure their stories
	Independent work Display the features checklists from earlier in the Unit for children to refer to as they are writing. You may also wish to generate a generic checklist for story writing – paragraphing, complex sentences, powerful verbs and so on. Children should begin writing their own stories independently, sticking to their plans from Day 4.	
Evaluation: judge effectiveness of own work	**Plenary** Children should self-assess their work; highlighting or using smiley faces where features from the checklist have been used. Ask them to think of one improvement they could work on in the next lesson.	

DAY 6 ■ Short story writing – opening, build-up

Key features	Stages	Additional opportunities
	Introduction Continue to model writing the short story from the plan incorporating organisational and language features of the genre, effective vocabulary choice, as well as modelled sentence construction and punctuation. Model the various stages of story writing, for example how to build up a story by developing characters, giving the reader clues to the problem.	**Support:** some children may need support in carrying out peer assessment or may benefit from the teacher suggesting the areas for improvement
Evaluation: give feedback to others	**Speaking and listening** Invite the children to work with a response partner to review writing from Day 5. They should read each other's stories. Using the checklists available, give partner feedback on where they have used the features of their chosen genre and generic story writing features and two areas for improvement.	
	Independent work Children should continue writing their own short stories independently, adhering to their plans and incorporating the language and organisational features from the checklists.	
	Plenary Children should self-assess against checklist of features for genre and/or generic narrative checklist. Assess whether they have addressed the improvements suggested by their response partner.	

DAY 7 ■ Short story writing - resolution, ending

Key features	Stages	Additional opportunities
	Introduction Continue to model writing the short story from the plan, incorporating organisational and language features of the genre, as well as modelled sentence construction and punctuation.	
Evaluation: give feedback to others	**Speaking and listening** Invite the children to work with a response partner to review writing from Day 6. They should read each other's stories, feedback on positive features and areas for improvement as in Day 6.	**ICT:** children may wish to present their stories using ICT or make individual or class books
	Independent work Ask the children to continue writing their own short stories independently.	
Evaluation: judge effectiveness of own work	**Plenary** Children should self-assess against checklist of features for genre and/or generic narrative checklist.	

DAY 8 ■ Evaluating stories

Key features	Stages	Additional opportunities
	Introduction Scan the work of a child who has covered lots of features from the lists, into a computer and display it. As a class, mark the piece together, noting where the writing is effective. For example: choice of vocabulary, powerful verbs, how writing has been organised (paragraphs, sentence construction), where features of the genre have been used and where improvements can be made – in grammar, organisation, use of language. Model the editing and re-drafting process.	
Evaluation: judge effectiveness of own work	**Independent work** Encourage the children to review their stories, re-drafting as necessary. Allow time for them to finish and publish their stories, either as handwritten books or word-processed.	
Evaluation: give feedback to others	**Plenary** Children should swap stories with a response partner, give feedback on positive aspects and one area for improvement.	

DAY 9 ■ Oral story telling

Key features	Stages	Additional opportunities
	Introduction Retell a short story orally to the children (it could be the one written together). Ask them to listen and watch for how you tell it. Create a checklist for oral story telling to be used by the audience in evaluating the stories heard. For example, if it is clear, audible, use of intonation, makes good sense, use of gesture, props and so on.	**Support:** some children may need to read their stories aloud from their books
Communication: communicate outcomes orally	**Independent work** Give children time to re-read their own stories and make notes if they wish, gather simple props and rehearse their stories with a friend. Invite children to retell their stories orally in small groups, using brief notes as an aide memoire if necessary. Encourage the children not to simply read out their stories from their books.	
	Plenary As a class, feed back on the features which made the most successful oral stories and what made it difficult. Make a class display or book of the short stories written.	

Guided reading

Continue to give children a range of experience of short story texts in different genre.

Assessment

Do the short stories demonstrate the features of the chosen genre?
Have the children used complex sentences, paragraphing and correct punctuation?
Identify next steps in writing.
Invite the children to complete the assessment activity 'Identifying genre' from the CD-ROM
Refer back to the learning outcomes on page 11.

Further work

Children could continue short story writing in a writing journal outside literacy lessons.
Use of reading journal to record responses to stories read.

Genre features

Fantasy

- Imaginary setting (such as a new land)
- Imaginary characters (such as monsters, trolls, magicians)
- Often one hero
- Plot is usually an adventure/quest involving a journey – the hero must find an object, defeat an evil creature…
- Language features – description of fantastical creatures, lands, invented vocabulary

Historical

- Set in the past (such as Roman times, Victorian times)
- Characters appropriate to the period of history (Roman soldiers, chimney sweep)
- Plot often based on fact
- Language features – style may reflect old English, include old-fashioned expressions, unfamiliar names for objects, places or people

Science fiction

- Setting – either familiar or another planet, galaxy
- Characters – aliens, unsuspecting hero
- Plot often based on the invasion of Earth or an unusual encounter
- Structure – opening, build-up, problem (encounter with aliens), conflict, resolution
- Language features – techniques used to create suspense, description used to describe aliens

Mystery

- Setting – generally familiar/crime scene
- Characters – realistic, detective, criminals
- Plot – logical, may include flashbacks/ shifts in time/believable resolution
- Clues – author provides clues throughout story to help solve crime
- Language features – sometimes written in the style of a private detective

100 LITERACY FRAMEWORK LESSONS YEAR 6

PHOTOCOPIABLE   ■SCHOLASTIC
www.scholastic.co.uk

Story ladder

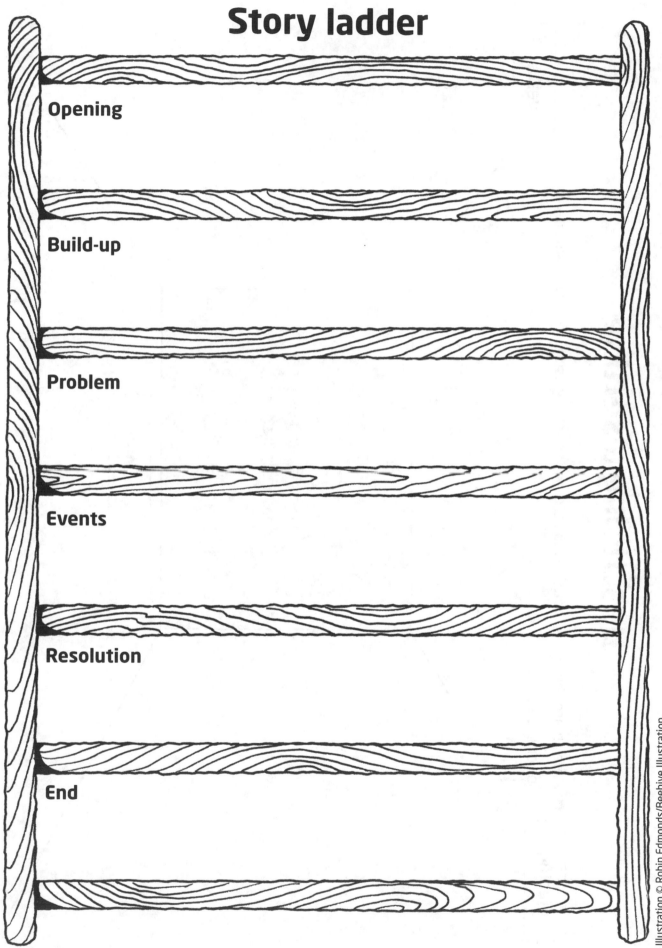

Opening

Build-up

Problem

Events

Resolution

End

Illustration © Robin Edmonds/Beehive Illustration.

Name _____   **Date** _____

Describing a setting

■ Write phrases below the headings to describe the setting using adjectives, adverbs and powerful verbs.

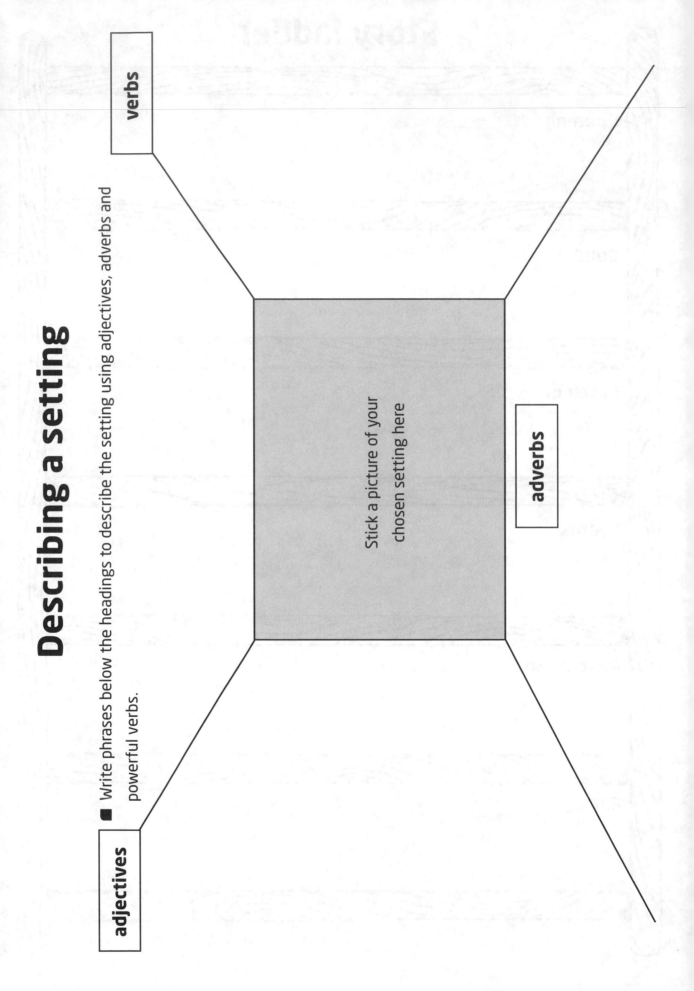

verbs

adjectives

adverbs

Stick a picture of your chosen setting here

NARRATIVE
UNIT 2 Extending narrative

Speak and listen for a range of purposes on paper and on screen

Strand 1 Speaking
- Use the techniques of dialogic talk to explore ideas, topics or issues.

Strand 4 Drama
- Improvise using a range of drama strategies and conventions to explore themes such as hopes, fears, desires.

Read for a range of purposes on paper and on screen

Strand 6 Word structure and spelling
- Use a range of appropriate strategies to edit, proofread and correct spelling in own work, on paper and on screen.

Strand 7 Understanding and interpreting texts
- Understand how writers use different structures to create coherence and impact.

Strand 8 Engaging with and responding to texts
- Sustain engagement with longer texts, using different techniques to make the text come alive.
- Compare how writers from different times and places present experiences and use language.

Write for a range of purposes on paper and on screen

Strand 9 Creating and shaping texts
- Set own challenges to extend achievement and experience in writing.
- Use different narrative techniques to engage and entertain the reader.
- Select words and language drawing on their knowledge of literary features and formal and informal writing.
- Integrate words, images and sounds imaginatively for different purposes.

Strand 10 Text structure and organisation
- Use varied structures to shape and organise texts coherently.

Strand 11 Sentence structure and punctuation
- Express subtle distinctions of meaning, including hypothesis, speculation and supposition, by constructing sentences in varied ways.
- Use punctuation to clarify meaning in complex sentences.

Strand 12 Presentation
- Use different styles of handwriting for different purposes with a range of media, developing consistent and personal legible style.
- Select from a wide range of ICT programs to present text effectively and communicate information and ideas.

Progression in narrative

In this year children are moving towards:
- Planning quickly and effectively the plot, characters and structure of own narrative writing; using paragraphs to vary pace and emphasis; varying sentence length to achieve a particular effect; using a variety of techniques to introduce characters and develop characterisation; using dialogue at key points.
- Creating a setting by: using expressive or figurative language; describing how it makes the character feel; adding detail of sights and sounds.
- Varying narrative structure when writing complete stories.

UNIT 2 ◄ Extending narrative *continued*

Key aspects of learning covered in this Unit

Enquiry
Children will assess information, pose questions and seek evidence to answer them.

Information processing
Children will respond to information from a range of sources on paper and on screen and compare, combine and orchestrate this as a basis for solving or completing an adventure text.

Evaluation
Children will share ideas, strategies and their consequences orally and in writing. They will discuss success criteria, give feedback to others and judge the effectiveness of their own and others' strategies and solutions in reading and creating an adventure text.

Reasoning
Children will construct reasoned arguments based on their views and responses to the text they read and create.

Problem solving
Children will take decisions based on available evidence, explore their consequences and adjust future decisions accordingly.

Empathy
In reading, writing or creating text adventures, children will explore techniques to enable them to imagine themselves in another person's position.

Self-awareness
Children will discuss and reflect on their personal responses to the texts.

Communication
Children will develop their ability to discuss and debate issues and personal responses; they will communicate outcomes orally.

Prior learning

Before starting this Unit check that the children can:
■ Identify and discuss the various features of a fiction text.
■ Discuss their responses to a range of fictional or imaginative texts they have read, on paper and on screen.
■ Know how various communication modes, for example visual images, video, sounds, can be used alongside or in combination with words to tell a story.
■ Know how to navigate an interactive non-linear (ICT) text.
■ Use a range of approaches and learning strategies to extend and explore their understanding of and response to a work of fiction.
If they need further support please refer to a prior Unit or a similar Unit in Year 5.

Resources

Phase 1:
Barrowquest story from the downloads section of: www.standards.dfes.gov.uk/primary/publications/literacy/63393; Photocopiable page 37 'Barrowquest story map'; Photocopiable page 38 'Identifying language and organisational features of Barrowquest'

Phase 2:
Photocopiable page 39 'Mythical land map'; Interactive activity 'Mythical land map'; Photocopiable page 40 'Blank story map'; Presentational software; Assessment activity 'Quest adventure stories' ❦

Cross-curricular opportunities

History (Ancient Greeks)

UNIT 2 ■ Teaching sequence

Phase	Children's objectives	Summary of activities	Learning outcomes
1	I can understand the structure of a multiple pathway quest story.	Examine the reading pathways in a multi-pathway quest story. Use role play to explore character. Construct a story map.	Children can read and analyse the structure of a multi pathway quest story.
2	I can plan and write a quest story. I can work collaboratively in a group.	Create a setting for a quest story. Work collaboratively to plan and write a quest story. Create an ICT-based text.	Children can plan and write a quest story collaboratively. Children can transfer their story into an interactive presentation, using ICT.

Provide copies of the objectives for the children.

DAY 1 ■ Introducing quest stories

Key features	Stages	Additional opportunities
	Introduction Read the opening chapter of *Barrowquest* from NLS exemplification Unit (see Downloads list from www.standards.dfes.gov.uk/primary/publications/literacy/ 63393). Note devices used by author to engage reader, introduce the hero and the situation. Establish that this is a quest adventure story: Lin has been chosen by his tribe to find the magician in order to save his people. Ask the children for other quest stories they know of – King Arthur, *Lord of the Rings*, Greek myths. Explain that this is a 'multiple choice text', it has different reading pathways. Show the children that at the end of chapter one, the reader can choose whether to go *North, South, East* or *West*.	
	Independent work Divide the class into four groups and give each group a different direction and the chapter relating to it. Ask the children to think about the features of the text – what do they notice?	**Support:** put children in groups with an adult
Communication: communicate outcomes orally	**Plenary** Ask each of the four groups to feed back on what happened in their chapter. Note how all four end in the same way as Lin is faced with four doors and the next choice of pathway. Begin completing photocopiable page 37 'Barrowquest story map', showing the organisation of the pathways.	

DAY 2 ■ Quest drama

Key features	Stages	Additional opportunities
	Introduction Tell the children they are going to imagine that they are Lin, the hero of the story, and that they are going to improvise his actions and movements.	
Empathy: imagine themselves in another person's position	**Speaking and listening** Provide the narration for the story while the children act it out. Begin with Lin being told he had to embark on the quest, entering the barrow and choosing between the stone passageways, and continue working through one of the chapters. Remind the children that Lin is a reluctant hero. At various intervals freeze-frame and ask the children in role about their fears, hopes, thoughts and physical feelings at that point in the story. Return to the text; vote on which reading pathway to take next. Read the next section, displaying the text, noting the devices used to engage the reader and language features.	**Extend:** improvise a different scene – for example, Lin being told he has to embark on the quest to help his people; or the children could form the setting (such as *the amazing roots*) while Lin attempts to navigate around them
	Plenary Discuss possible ideas for the challenge Lin could face in the next chapter. Encourage the children to think about the sort of challenges and puzzles encountered by quest heroes. Update the story map begun in Day 1.	

DAY 3 ■ Choosing pathways

Key features	Stages	Additional opportunities
	### Introduction As a class, choose the next chapter to read. Analyse the language and organisational features of the text – setting, magical elements, hero, dangers and puzzles encountered, how the author uses complex and short sentences for effect, building of tension, language choices (adverbs, verbs and so on), character's thoughts and feelings, clues about the quest. At the next reading pathway choice, allow children to choose their own pathway and give out copies of the text.	
	### Independent work Children read chosen pathways independently or in small groups with an adult. Give the children photocopiable page 38, 'Identifying language and organisational features of Barrowquest', to complete while reading.	**Support:** some groups may need to work with an adult or be given a simpler text
Communication: communicate outcomes orally	### Plenary Discuss the different endings to the quest adventure. Complete the story map which you have been filling in. Review the structure of a quest story – reason for quest, journey, the dangers encountered, successful resolution. Note how each chapter contains a 'mini quest'. Ask the children to give examples of the language and organisational features found during their independent work.	

Guided reading
Use the *Barrowquest* text and allow groups to explore other reading pathways.

Assessment
Can the children identify the features of a quest story?
Can the children construct a visual map of the story?
Refer back to the learning outcomes on page 29.

Further work
A computer-based multimodal quest adventure game could be used as an alternative or in addition to this story. Write alternative chapters for the *Barrowquest* story.

DAY 1 ■ Planning a quest

Key features	Stages	Additional opportunities
Evaluation: discuss success criteria	**Introduction** Tell children they are going to write a class quest adventure story. Create a checklist of what makes a successful quest story – object/person to be searched for, stock characters (such as knights, magicians or trolls), tasks, obstacles, harsh mythical land, successful resolution. Take possible ideas for a quest plot.	
	Independent work Organise the children into four groups. Each group should draw a section of a map of a mythical land, for example North, South, East and West. Add in physical features such as volcanoes, a dragon's den, underground caves, rivers, rope bridges and mythical, fearsome creatures. (Alternatively, the map of a mythical land on photocopiable page 39 could be provided for the children to explore and add to.)	**Extend:** begin generating description of their setting **Support:** use the interactive Mythical map from the CD-ROM
Evaluation: share ideas	**Plenary** Ask each group to explain their part of the land to the rest of the class. Encourage questions. Show children a selection of objects or people (cup, lamp, map, treasure chest and so on) and ask them to vote as a class as to which object or person their quest will be for.	

DAY 2 ■ Beginning the quest

Key features	Stages	Additional opportunities
	Introduction Recap on the previous lesson and the object or person the class quest story is to be built around.	
	Speaking and listening In pairs, ask the children to discuss the purpose of the quest – to save people, to free a prisoner, to appease an evil ruler. Invite pairs to feed back ideas to the class, decide which one to use for the class story. Remind children of the *Barrowquest* story map, and give them a copy of photocopiable page 40 'Blank story map'. Model writing the opening chapter of the class story establishing the setting, the purpose of the quest and introducing the character(s). Model using the techniques identified in Phase 1 to engage the reader. End the chapter with four reading pathways. Involve the children through shared composition using individual whiteboards.	
Communication: discuss issues	**Plenary** Divide the children into groups of four. Explain that they are going to continue the class quest story, each writing a different pathway. Allow them to explore some possible ideas for the next chapter.	

DAY 3 ■ Group quests

Key features	Stages	Additional opportunities
	Introduction Remind the children that they are writing a quest story in groups of four, based around the idea decided on by the class and using the chapter written in Day 2 as the opening chapter. In their groups of four, each child will write four further chapters.	
Evaluation: share ideas	**Speaking and listening** Allow time for the groups to discuss what will happen in each pathway and what their finishing point for chapter 2 will be (for example, the hero finds himself with four doors to choose from, four roads, four tunnels).	
	Independent work Children work independently, writing their versions of chapter 2, the start of the journey. Encourage them to use the language and organisational features identified in *Barrowquest* (build up of suspense, vivid descriptions, character's thoughts and feelings). Remind children of quest story features.	**ICT:** this work could be done straight on to computer, if available, using presentational software
Evaluation: give feedback to others	**Plenary** Children re-form into their groups and share their progress so far, swapping chapters and ensuring that they all finish at the same point. There is an opportunity for peer assessment here.	

DAY 4 ■ Inventing pathways

Key features	Stages	Additional opportunities
	Introduction Scan one child's version of chapter 2 into a computer to read as a class, highlighting the use of language and organisational features. At the end of the chapter, establish that the reader now has another choice of pathway. (Children should have decided on these pathways in the previous lesson.) Tell the children that the next chapter should involve the hero encountering a hostile creature and defeating it. Model writing the start of a version of chapter 3.	
Evaluation: share ideas	**Speaking and listening** In writing groups, children decide on four different encounters for chapter 3 (such as a dragon, a troll, giant ants and a bear). The groups should decide on the finishing point and their next four choices (for example, the finding of a magic object, playing an instrument, solving a riddle).	**ICT:** this work could be done straight on to computer, if available, using presentational software
	Independent work Children should work independently, writing their versions of chapter 3.	
Evaluation: give feedback to others	**Plenary** Children re-form into groups and share progress so far, swapping chapters and ensuring that they all finish at the same point. There is an opportunity for peer assessment here.	

DAY 5 ■ Overcoming obstacles

Key features	Stages	Additional opportunities
	Introduction Recap on the story structure by referring to the story map constructed in Phase 1. Remind children of the setting they created with their map and discuss where the hero could go next, what obstacles they might encounter on the way, any difficult terrain. Collect ideas. Establish that in chapter 4 the hero must overcome another obstacle. Model writing a version of chapter 4, incorporating the language and organisational features of quest stories. Model the construction of complex sentences and effective use of punctuation.	**Support:** help children with the construction of complex sentences
	Speaking and listening Ask the groups to decide on the next four pathways and the finishing point for the chapter.	
	Independent work The children should continue writing chapters 3 and 4 of their quest story in their groups of four (allow for children working at different speeds).	**ICT:** this work could be done straight on to computer, if available, using presentational software
Communication: communicate outcomes orally	**Plenary** In groups, share progress so far. Check that their story is fitting into the story map, that there is continuity in the story and that all chapters are finishing at the same point.	

DAY 6 ■ Completing the quest

Key features	Stages	Additional opportunities
	Introduction Explain that chapter 5 is the final chapter of the story. This chapter must involve the hero finding the treasure (either the object or person). It may involve them confronting a guardian or the final danger and the significance of the treasure will be revealed. It should also involve the hero returning home and an explanation of what happens there, thus resolving the story. Discuss possible endings for their quest stories.	**Extend:** experiment with choosing different pathways through their own stories
	Speaking and listening Allow groups to evaluate their progress and to decide what they still need to achieve.	
Evaluation: discuss success criteria	**Independent work** Allow time for independent writing of any outstanding chapters and of chapter 5. Make the story map structure and writing checklists available.	
	Plenary Review progress in groups, check continuity of their stories.	

DAY 7 ◼ Planning an interactive quest

Key features	Stages	Additional opportunities
	Introduction Show the children how to organise their story into an ICT-based presentation using presentational software. Each slide of the presentation should display one chapter. Demonstrate how to insert four button links at the bottom of each slide – one for each pathway choice. This will enable the reader to choose their pathway. Show the children how to import digital photographs or clip-art, sounds or video clips (copyright permitting) to accompany their story.	
Empathy: imagine themselves in another person's position	**Speaking and listening** As a group, children should create a plan of how to translate their stories into ICT-based adventure texts deciding on graphics and sounds, font and so on. They could create a storyboard with outline sketches of their ideas.	**Support:** it may be useful if the text for the stories is already available as a word-processed document
	Independent work Allow time for finishing the writing of the stories, editing and beginning ICT work.	
Evaluation: discuss success criteria	**Plenary** Model the editing and re-drafting of one chapter either from the class story or one of the group stories, using the checklist of features and ensuring good use of grammar. Discuss appropriate graphics, music, sound, fonts to use in presentation of this chapter.	

DAY 8 ◼ Publishing a quest adventure

Key features	Stages	Additional opportunities
	Introduction Remind the children of the story they have been creating. Tell them that today they will be continuing their ICT presentations.	
	Independent work Encourage groups to organise themselves to work on writing, re-drafting and publishing to produce a finished ICT-based multimodal text. This will involve typing up text, importing pictures and adding sound files (copyright permitting). Depending on the package used, children can create buttons on their slides which allow them to navigate through different pathway choices. Work may need to be carried on outside the literacy lesson.	**Support:** allocate roles to children
	Plenary Each group should end up with a complete ICT-based multiple choice text. As the children work on this, ask them to display their work in progress and discuss their reasons behind decisions made.	

DAY 9 ■ Evaluating quests

Key features	Stages	Additional opportunities
	### Introduction Recap on features of quest adventure stories. As a class create an evaluation sheet for the stories incorporating: ■ Structure – does it follow the story map? ■ Continuity – do the chapters all finish at the same point? ■ Language features – vivid description, tension created ■ Plot – quest for object/person ■ Setting and characters appropriate to quest ■ Visual appeal of presentation ■ Ease of navigation between chapters ■ Motivation for reader.	**Support:** a teacher-prepared evaluation sheet could be provided for the children to use
	### Speaking and listening Children present their finished ICT-based quest stories to the rest of the class, allowing them to decide on the reading pathway. This could be done either in an ICT suite with children working in pairs on individual computers or as a whole class using an interactive whiteboard for presenting. The audience should complete an evaluation sheet.	
Evaluation: give feedback to others	### Plenary Give groups their own story evaluation sheets. Invite another class or parents to view quest adventure stories.	

Guided reading
Chapters written by the children could be used for guided reading, allowing an opportunity to evaluate and suggest improvements.
ICT-based multimodal texts could be used in guided reading.

Assessment
Can the children work collaboratively to write a quest story?
Can the children create stories using the features of quest stories?
Can the children complete a plausible story map?
Complete the CD-ROM assessment activity 'Quest adventure stories'.
Refer back to the learning outcomes on page 29.

Further work
Stories could be shared with other classes.
Further work could be carried out in ICT lessons using digital cameras, video, creating sound files, recording stories read aloud.

Name _____ Date _____

Barrowquest story map

■ As you read *Barrowquest*, fill in the boxes of the story map with a summary of events in each chapter.

Chapter 1

Chapter 2 North	**Chapter 2** South	**Chapter 2** East	**Chapter 2** West

Chapter 3 Oak	**Chapter 3** Ash	**Chapter 3** Elm	**Chapter 3** Thorn

Chapter 4 Harp	**Chapter 4** Flute	**Chapter 4** Tambourine	**Chapter 4** Lute

Chapter 5 Blue	**Chapter 5** Green	**Chapter 5** Indigo	**Chapter 5** Violet

Identifying language and organisational features of Barrowquest

■ From your reading of *Barrowquest*, find examples of the following features of quest stories.

Content	
Location	
Danger or puzzle	
Magical elements	
Language features	
Building tension	
Character's thoughts	
Powerful verbs	
Adjectives	
Adverbs	
Complex sentences	
Short sentences	

Mythical land map

■ Explore and add to this map.

NARRATIVE ■ UNIT 2

Blank story map

■ Use the blank story map to plan your group's quest adventure.

Chapter 1

Chapter 2	Chapter 2	Chapter 2	Chapter 2

Chapter 3	Chapter 3	Chapter 3	Chapter 3

Chapter 4	Chapter 4	Chapter 4	Chapter 4

Chapter 5	Chapter 5	Chapter 5	Chapter 5

NARRATIVE
UNIT 3 Authors and texts

Speak and listen for a range of purposes on paper and on screen

Strand 1 Speaking
- Use a range of oral techniques to present persuasive arguments and engaging narratives.
- Use the techniques of dialogic talk to explore ideas, topics or issues.

Strand 3 Group discussion and interaction
- Understand and use a variety of ways to criticise constructively and respond to criticism.

Strand 4 Drama
- Improvise using a range of drama strategies and conventions to explore themes such as hopes, fears, desires.

Read for a range of purposes on paper and on screen

Strand 6 Word structure and spelling
- Spell familiar words correctly and employ a range of strategies to spell difficult and unfamiliar words.
- Use a range of appropriate strategies to edit, proofread and correct spelling in their own work, on paper and on screen.

Strand 8 Engaging with and responding to texts
- Read extensively and discuss personal reading with others, including in reading groups.
- Sustain engagement with longer texts, using different techniques to make the text come alive.

Write for a range of purposes on paper and on screen

Strand 9 Creating and shaping texts
- Set their own challenges to extend achievement and experience in writing.
- Use different narrative techniques to engage and entertain the reader.

Strand 10 Text structure and organisation
- Use varied structures to shape and organise texts coherently.
- Use paragraphs to achieve pace and emphasis.

Strand 11 Sentence structure and punctuation
- Express subtle distinctions of meaning, including hypothesis, speculation and supposition, by constructing sentences in varied ways.
- Use punctuation to clarify meaning in complex sentences.

Strand 12 Presentation
- Use different styles of handwriting for different purposes with a range of media, developing a consistent and personal legible style.
- Select from a wide range of ICT programs to present text effectively and communicate information and ideas.

Progression in narrative

In this year children are moving towards:
- Looking at elements of an author's style to identify common elements and then make comparisons between books; considering how style is influenced by the time when they wrote and the intended audience; recognising that the narrator can change and be manipulated and talking about the effect this has.

▶

UNIT 3 ◀ Authors and texts *continued*

Key aspects of learning covered in this Unit

Enquiry
Children will identify their own key questions about the work of a particular writer, and then locate the evidence to answer them.

Information processing
Children will respond to information or stimuli from a range of sources on paper and on screen and compare, combine and orchestrate this as a basis for both oral and written communication

Evaluation
Children will share responses orally and in writing. They will discuss success criteria, give feedback to others and judge the effectiveness of their own work.

Reasoning
Children will construct reasoned arguments based on their views and responses to the books or stories read.

Empathy
In discussing and writing about the books or stories, children will need to imagine themselves in another person's position. They will explore techniques that facilitate this process.

Communication
Children will develop their ability to discuss and debate issues and personal responses both in respect of the form and the content of the stories they are reading and the journal they are creating. They will often work collaboratively in pairs and groups. They will communicate outcomes orally, in writing and through other modes and media.

Prior learning

Before starting this Unit check that the children can:
■ Identify and discuss the various features of a fiction text.
■ Discuss their responses to a range of fiction they have read.
■ Use a range of approaches and learning strategies, for example role play, dialogue and experimental writing, to extend and explore their understanding of and response to a work of fiction.
If they need further support please refer to a prior Unit or a similar Unit in Year 5.

Resources

Phase 1:
Pig-Heart Boy by Malorie Blackman (Doubleday); *Pig-Heart Boy Extracts 1, 2 and 3* ✺; Photocopiable page 53 'Character web'
Phase 2:
Pig-Heart Boy by Malorie Blackman (Doubleday); Sound or video recording equipment; Computers with access to internal email or instant messenger
Phase 3:
Pig-Heart Boy by Malorie Blackman (Doubleday); Digital camera; Presentational software
Phase 4:
Photocopiable page 54 'Reading journal activities'; Assessment activity 'Pig-Heart Boy' ✺

Cross-curricular opportunities

PSHE links – bullying, animal rights

UNIT 3 ■ Teaching sequence

Phase	Children's objectives	Summary of activities	Learning outcomes
1	I understand what logs and journals are used for.	Construct an argument from a character's viewpoint. Write the transcript for an interview with a journalist. Create a character web.	Children can record their responses to a novel in a variety of ways.
2	I can explore the conflicts between characters using drama techniques.	Explore the relationship between two characters. Simulate a conversation between the characters using email or instant messaging. Create a diary entry using a sound/video file.	Children can explore conflicts between characters using drama and reading journal.
3	I can explore relationships between characters and record my responses in writing.	Re-write extract from a different narrative viewpoint. Use freeze-framing to explore an episode in the story.	Children can use drama techniques and a range of writing forms to record their responses to a text.
4	I can demonstrate how to use a reading journal to help me respond to a text.	Evaluate reading journal. Create a guide to using reading journal.	Children can reflect upon the use of reading journal and evaluate them against a checklist.

Provide copies of the objectives for the children.

DAY 1 ■ Logs and journals

Key features	Stages	Additional opportunities
Communication: discuss issues	**Introduction** Ensure that the class has read, or heard, *Pig-Heart Boy* by Malorie Blackman, before starting the Unit. Discuss the use of logs, journal, weblogs (to record events, as an outlet for emotions, to communicate with others and so on). You may wish to read a range of examples from novels and other media (for example, *The Wreck of the Zanzibar* by Michael Morpurgo, *The Suitcase Kid* by Jacqueline Wilson, weblogs on the internet). Ask the children to think about why people keep logs, journal, diaries. Collect ideas. Remind them about the video diary Cameron creates in *Pig-Heart Boy* for his unborn sibling. Ask the children to think about why he does this.	
	Independent work Read, either on screen or on paper, examples of logs or journals. Identify the audience and purpose of these logs.	**Support:** groups could be assigned authors and texts
Enquiry: identify key questions about the work of a particular writer	**Plenary** Organise children into groups. In their groups, ask children to select another well known children's author and each agree to read one book by that author in order to write a synopsis and present to the rest of the group at the end of the Unit. They may need to be given a list to choose from.	

DAY 2 ■ Reading journal

Key features	Stages	Additional opportunities
	Introduction Introduce the use of a reading journal to record, explore and respond to books that have been read. Re-read Chapters 1 and 2 of *Pig-Heart Boy*. Discuss how Malorie Blackman introduces the character Cameron, his illness and his feelings by showing the contrast between him and his friends at the swimming pool. Pick out evidence from the text that shows how he feels about his illness and his inability to do what the other children can do.	
Reasoning: construct reasoned arguments based on books read	**Speaking and listening** Ask the children to work in pairs to create a debate. Half the class should construct an argument from Cameron's point of view – arguing why he should be allowed to go swimming despite his condition. The other half can construct an argument from his friends' or parents' point of view – arguing why he should not be allowed to go swimming due to his condition. Record arguments in reading journals.	**Support:** provide adult support
Communication: debate issues	**Plenary** Join pairs into groups of four to present their arguments. Children could record the opposing argument in their reading journal also.	

DAY 3 ▪ Character webs

Key features	Stages	Additional opportunities
	Introduction Read *Pig-Heart Boy Extracts* 2 and 3 from the CD-ROM. Discuss how the author uses the video diary as a device to convey the honest feelings of the character to the reader – about his illness, parents, a girl he likes at school. Model drawing a character web showing Cameron's relationship with the other characters in the book. On the lines between the characters, write down how they feel about each other, any tensions and so on.	
Empathy: imagine themselves in another person's position	**Independent work** Encourage children to work with response partners to draw their own character web for Cameron showing his relationship to the other characters and the nature of those relationships or use photocopiable page 53 'Character web' and add to it. For extension, children could also show the relationships between the other characters on their web (for example, Mum and Dr Ehrlich, Mum and Dad).	**Support:** provide statements about relationships for the children to match to characters, such as *she doesn't trust him* or *she always listens to him*
Communication: work collaboratively in pairs	**Plenary** Ask children to swap partners and to explain a character web to them.	

DAY 4 ▪ Reporters

Key features	Stages	Additional opportunities
Communication: communicate outcomes orally	**Introduction** Remind the children of the point in the story when Cameron has had his heart operation (Chapter 13). Read *Pig-Heart Boy Extract 1* from the CD-ROM as a prompt. Ask them to imagine they are newspaper reporters and to think about what questions they would like to ask him. Children could talk to response partners to think of a question. Collect the responses. Discuss with the children how they think Cameron might answer the questions. You could role play the interview.	
Information processing: respond to information	**Independent work** Using their reading journal, ask the children to write the transcript of an interview between a reporter and Cameron, either for television or for a newspaper.	**Extend:** act out their television or newspaper interviews
	Plenary Re-read the extract from the story where Cameron is involved in a television interview (Chapter 16). Compare this to the interviews written by the children.	

Guided reading

Re-read extracts from the novel in guided reading time.

Read extracts from other journals, diaries, logs.

Assessment

Can children describe ways in which journal, diaries and logs can be used?

Can children record their responses to the novel in a variety of ways, through use of a reading journal?

Refer back to the learning outcomes on page 43.

Further work

The interviews between Cameron and a reporter could be role played.

Other ideas for reading journal – letters to or from characters, character description, poem about character, newspaper articles, diary entries.

DAY 1 ■ Friendship

Key features	Stages	Additional opportunities
	Introduction Explore the relationship between Cameron and Marlon and subsequent conflict when Marlon's parents sell Cameron's story to the newspaper. Re-read extracts that reveal the closeness of their friendship – when Cameron confides in Marlon about his operation, Marlon protects him from other children and so on. Then, re-read the extract when the newspaper article is revealed. Explore Cameron's feelings of betrayal and Marlon's explanation.	
Empathy: imagine themselves in another person's position	**Independent work** Encourage children to work with a partner to record in a journal the point of view of the two boys at various places in the story. Give parts of the story to consider, for example: ■ At the start of their swimming trip ■ Just before the operation ■ After the operation ■ When the newspaper article appears ■ Marlon's apology ■ Swimming trip. Children may record the characters' thoughts at some or all of these points.	**Support:** just consider Marlon's or Cameron's point of view or consider one point in the story only
Communication: communicate outcomes orally	**Plenary** Invite children to share the characters' thoughts and feelings at different points in the story.	

DAY 2 ■ Best friends?

Key features	Stages	Additional opportunities
	Introduction Decide on a point in the story to work from, such as when Cameron discovers the newspaper article about his operation or his first day back at school after the operation. Discuss the conversation Cameron and Marlon might have at this point; use the reflections from Day 1. It may be useful to write down the exchanges that the two boys would have – for example, as a playscript, text messages or emails.	
Empathy: imagine themselves in another person's position	**Independent work** Organise the children to work in pairs, one in role as Cameron and one in role as Marlon. Using separate computers, pairs simulate an email or instant messaging conversation between the two characters at this point in the story.	**ICT:** if an ICT suite is not available, children could role play the conversations either as an improvisation or by first scripting them
Evaluation: share responses	**Plenary** Reflect, in role, on the impact of the simulated conversation on their thoughts and feelings towards the other character; record them in reading journals. Those children finding this difficult may need questions given to them to respond to or could simply record the other character's viewpoint. Share some reflections.	

DAY 3 ■ Exploring conflict

Key features	Stages	Additional opportunities
	## Introduction Remind children how Cameron uses a video diary to record his thoughts and feelings. Ask the children to choose a scenario of their own based on the theme of conflict between friends (for example, a betrayal or misunderstanding). Children make notes on their invented scenario. Model writing notes for a character, explaining their feelings (based on one of the invented scenarios). What sort of things would they include in their video diary? Using these notes, invite a confident child to create a video file or sound recording, in role, for one of the characters in the scenario.	
Empathy: imagine themselves in another person's position **Evaluation:** feedback to others	## Independent work Children should write, rehearse and record a video/sound diary entry for a chosen character in their scenario. They may find it helpful to re-read extracts from the novel when preparing for this. ## Plenary Everyone should watch/listen to the different recordings, evaluate and feed back. Did the entries convey the situation and the characters' feelings? What else would they want to ask the character?	**Extend:** consider how this work could be used to create a written piece, such as a diary entry

Guided reading
Read extracts from *Pig-Heart Boy* or other Malorie Blackman novels, such as *Hacker, Thief, Noughts and Crosses* or *A.N.T.I.D.O.T.E.*

Assessment
Can children effectively use drama techniques to explore the conflict between characters?
Refer back to the learning outcomes on page 43.

Further work
Reading journal ideas: choosing favourite extract, drawing character, letters to and from characters or someone such as a neighbour, a teacher, the police, book review, opinions based on reading, turn a section into a playscript or write a summary of the story in 50 words.

DAY 1 ■ Narrative viewpoint

Key features	Stages	Additional opportunities
	Introduction Introduce the idea of narrative viewpoint and discuss the effect of writing the book in the first person – from Cameron's point of view. Re-read Chapter 3; discuss the impact of having Mum and Dad's argument overheard by Cameron. Model rewriting the beginning of the episode from either Mum or Dad's point of view. Establish the use of other words for *said*, similes, actions, thoughts and speech to create the atmosphere and build up the tension. As a class, discuss other scenarios which include conflict – between parents, siblings and friends. You may allow children time to talk to response partners, collect their ideas.	
	Independent work Ask the children to plan a story based on the theme of conflict. Ask them to select a main character from whose viewpoint the story will be written and to construct a character web showing their relationship to other characters in the story. Allow children time throughout the Unit, and outside the literacy lesson, to work on their own extended narrative.	**Support:** provide a writing frame or structure
Communication: communicate outcomes orally	**Plenary** Encourage children to explain their plans and character webs to another child.	

DAY 2 ■ Freeze-frames

Key features	Stages	Additional opportunities
	Introduction Re-read Cameron's homecoming from Chapter 15. Explore how Cameron and his parents feel, why the reporters are there, whether their actions are justified, what the children think they should do/the police should do.	
Empathy: imagine themselves in another person's position	**Speaking and listening** Create a freeze-frame enactment of this chapter and take digital photographs (ensure to get parents' or carers' permission before taking photographs) – in the car, arriving home to reporters, being inside house, telephone calls, receiving letters from animal rights activists. Question children in role during freeze-framing: *Why are you here? What do you think about using animal hearts for transplants? How do you feel? Do you think your actions are justified?* Some of the children could re-enact the scene while others construct and ask the questions.	
Communication: discuss and debate issues	**Plenary** Hot-seat a child in character as a reporter or activist. Time may need to be given to allow for children to write questions for the characters. Allow children time to work on their own conflict narratives which were planned in Day 1, for example in guided reading time/homework.	**Support:** provide questions

DAY 3 ■ Speech and thought bubbles

Key features	Stages	Additional opportunities
	Introduction Import digital images from Day 2 into a slideshow presentation. Model creating thought or speech bubbles for the characters in the scenes or use the images as a stimulus for writing complex sentences or short paragraphs.	
Evaluation: share responses	**Speaking and listening** Allow children to work with a partner, discussing and writing appropriate thought or speech bubble captions on individual whiteboards. Collect and use the children's ideas, model writing.	
	Independent work Load the slideshow on all the computers in an ICT suite. In pairs or independently, children should work on the slideshow presentation creating thought/speech bubble captions or writing paragraphs about the scenes. Alternatively, give the children copies of the photographs to work from on paper.	
	Plenary Allow children to move around ICT suite to view each others' presentations or present them to the class as a show. Children could assess each others' writing, for complex sentences, effective vocabulary and so on. Allow the children to work on their own conflict narratives – for example, in guided reading/homework.	

Guided reading

Read further extracts from *Pig-Heart Boy* or other Malorie Blackman novels such as *Hacker, Thief, Noughts and Crosses* or *A.N.T.I.D.O.T.E.*

Assessment

Can the children use drama techniques to explore conflicts in stories?
Do children understand the impact on the reader of narrative viewpoint?
Refer back to the learning outcomes on page 43.

Further work

Explore the relationship between Cameron and his Nan.
Explore the point of view of animal rights activists.
Use freeze-framing for another part of the story, for example Cameron's return to school.
Analyse Cameron's video diary entries.
Explore other work by Malorie Blackman.
Children can read their own book of choice for synopsis writing and presentation.
Allow children to work on own narratives (for example, in guided reading).

DAY 1 ■ Reflecting on reading

Key features	Stages	Additional opportunities
	Introduction Create with the children a list of possible ways of recording reflections in a reading journal – include writing raps, poems, character descriptions, interviews, playscripts, newspaper articles, letters to the author/to characters and favourite extracts. Encourage the children to give suggestions. They might also find it helpful to have photocopiable page 54 'Reading journal activities'.	
Enquiry: identify key questions about the work of a particular writer	**Independent work** Allow children to choose one of these recording methods to reflect on the book they have been reading by another author (chosen at the start of the Unit). They should create an entry for their reading journal based on their book.	**Extend:** use more than one method for reflecting on the book they have read **Support:** children could draw and label something from their book
Evaluation: discuss success criteria	**Plenary** Create a checklist for evaluation of reading journals. This is to be used in the selection of entries for a class reading journal. It could include creativity, empathy, uses evidence from the text, informative, presentation, variety of methods of recording and so on.	

DAY 2 ■ Evaluating reading journals

Key features	Stages	Additional opportunities
	Introduction Refer to the checklist for evaluating reading journals. Model evaluating a couple of reading journal entries together – scanned into a computer, using the checklist the children have created. Tell the children they are going to evaluate each others' journals and select entries for inclusion in a class anthology.	
Evaluation: give feedback to others	**Independent work** Children should swap reading journals with a partner for evaluation. Ask them to identify the features used effectively and entries in the journal that best fit the criteria on the checklist to nominate for the class anthology.	**Extend:** self-assess their journals
	Plenary Children should feed back to partners on what they did well, what would make them even better and the piece that they felt best fitted the criteria. Use the children's selections to create a class reading journal to be shown to other classes and parents.	

DAY 3 ■ Author reviews

Key features	Stages	Additional opportunities
	Introduction Ask the children to discuss, either as a class or with response partners, how the reading journals have helped them to understand, explore and reflect on a text. Write a class description of how to use a reading journal, include a list of possible ways of recording for someone who has never used one. This could go in the front of their journals or be displayed in the classroom.	
	Independent work Write a synopsis of the book selected for reading at the start of the Unit. In groups, either present or allow time for sharing synopses. Work with other group members on a short presentation about their author, intended to persuade others to read his/her books. They may contain reference to the plots, characters, writing style, overall effect on the reader.	**Support:** this activity could be used as an opportunity to recap on persuasive techniques
Evaluation: share responses orally	**Plenary** Groups or nominated children should present to the class on their author. When all of the presentations have been heard, ask the children if they have been persuaded to read one of the other authors' books based on the presentation.	

Guided reading
Read each other's reading journals and assess/evaluate them.

Assessment
Can the children explain how to use a reading journal and why it is useful? Complete the CD-ROM assessment activity 'Pig-Heart Boy'. Refer back to the learning outcomes on page 43.

Further work
Continue to write reading journal entries for other texts read either in class or independently.
Write book reviews based on independent reading.
Complete narratives based on theme of conflict.

Character web

■ Make a comment regarding the relationship between each character along each arrow. You will need to rotate the page.

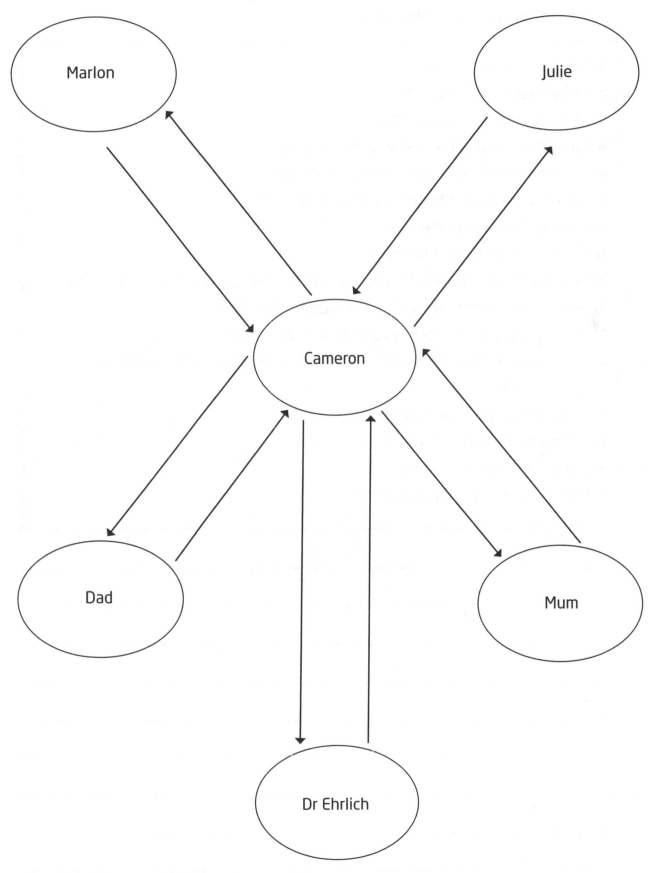

Name _____   Date _____

Reading journal activities

■ Pick one of the reading journal activites from the list below. When you have completed the activity, write why you chose the activity, what you enjoyed about it and what you learned from doing it on the lines below.

- Create a new book cover.
- Write a letter to a character.
- Write a letter from a character.
- Write the conversation between two characters.
- Write an interview with one of the characters.
- Create a storyboard to turn the book into a film.
- Write a playscript of the story.
- Rewrite the ending of the story.
- Create a character web showing the relationships between the characters.
- Write a newspaper article about an event in the story.
- Write a poem, rap or song about the book or a character.
- Pick out your favourite description and say why it is your favourite, and give examples.
- Write a description of your favourite character.
- Draw your favourite character.
- Draw a map of the setting.
- Write a diary entry for a character.

_____
_____
_____
_____
_____
_____
_____
_____
_____

NARRATIVE
UNIT 4 Short stories with flashbacks

Speak and listen for a range of purposes on paper and on screen

Strand 1 Speaking
■ Use a range of oral techniques to present persuasive arguments and engaging narratives.
Strand 2 Listening and responding
■ Make notes when listening for a sustained period and discuss how note-taking varies depending on context and purpose.

Read for a range of purposes on paper and on screen

Strand 6 Word structure and spelling
■ Use a range of appropriate strategies to edit, proofread and correct spelling in own work, on paper and on screen.
Strand 7 Understanding and interpreting texts
■ Understand how writers use different structures to create coherence and impact.
■ Understand underlying themes, causes and points of view.

Write for a range of purposes on paper and on screen

Strand 9 Creating and shaping texts
■ Use different narrative techniques to engage and entertain the reader.
■ Integrate words, images and sounds imaginatively for different purposes.
Strand 10 Text structure and organisation
■ Use varied structures to shape and organise texts coherently.

Progression in narrative

In this year children are moving towards:
■ Understanding different episodes (in story and on film) can take place in different settings; discussing why and how the scene changes are made and how they affect the characters and events; recognising that authors use language carefully to influence the reader's view of a place or situation.

UNIT 4 ◄ Short stories with flashbacks *continued*

Key aspects of learning covered in this Unit

Creative thinking
Children will generate ideas for a short narrative in response to a piece of music.

Reasoning
Children will discuss a short narrative film and give their opinions about the authorial intent, drawing inferences and making deductions from the text.

Empathy
Children will identify triggers and causes of other people's emotions.

Evaluation
Children will make judgements and justify their views and opinions, drawing on sources to support their evaluations. Children will discuss success criteria, give feedback to others and judge the effectiveness of their own work.

Information processing
Children will explore information communicated through different modes and use this to create their own narrative.

Prior learning

Before starting this Unit check that the children can:
■ Form opinions and personal responses to text, using evidence from a written or visual text to support and justify responses.
■ Infer authors' perspectives and understand underlying themes.
■ Use and manipulate paragraphs to structure and shape a narrative.
If they need further support please refer to a prior Unit or a similar Unit in Year 5.

Resources

Phase 1:
Hajj Extract 1 and *2* by Vince Cross ❦
Phase 2:
Piece of music such as *Aquarium* by Saint Saens; Photocopiable page 66 'Paragraph planner'; Presentation software; Photocopiable page 67 'Sentence surgery'; Photocopiable page 68 'Visual storyboard'; Assessment activity 'What's the mood?' ❦

Cross-curricular opportunities

History - World War 2

UNIT 4 ◼ Teaching sequence

Phase	Children's objectives	Summary of activities	Learning outcomes
1	I can identify how an author has created the mood of a text and how an author indicates shifts in time.	Devise and answer questions for a character. Write a story review. Make a story graph.	Children can identify how the author has used a range of techniques to create the mood of a text and to indicate shifts in time.
2	I can plan and write a narrative which conveys mood and shifts in time.	Plan a narrative piece using a paragraph planner. Set narrative to music. Sentence construction. Write narrative from an alternative viewpoint. Select visual images to accompany narrative. Review/evaluate work.	Children can plan and write a narrative, using paragraphs to structure their writing and create pace, and using a range of techniques to indicate mood and shifts in time.

Provide copies of the objectives for the children.

DAY 1 ◼ Story opening

Key features	Stages	Additional opportunities
Reasoning: make deductions from the text	**Introduction** Read *Hajj Extract 1* from the CD-ROM. Discuss the impact of the opening, how the narrator is feeling, and pick out the dramatic descriptions of the nightmare. Establish that the story is in the past tense, first person, and that the author is using flashback to tell the story. Ask the children what the *Virginia* is, what they think may have happened and who the characters are. Encourage them to use evidence from the text. **Speaking and listening** Ask the children to discuss in pairs who they think the narrator is, how old he is, and how he feels about events. Share some ideas with the class. **Independent work** Independently or in response partners, children should work to devise questions they would like to ask the narrator/main character. **Plenary** Share some of the questions devised. As a class, try to answer them, using evidence from the text. Establish how many characters there are in the story.	

DAY 2 ◼ Creating mood

Key features	Stages	Additional opportunities
	Introduction Display and recap on the opening of the story *Hajj*. Draw a character web, establishing what we already know about the characters. Establish the mood of the story so far (tense, awkward, guilty). Picking out evidence from the text, show how the author creates the mood (through character's thoughts, actions, short sentences, vocabulary). **Speaking and listening** In response partners, ask children to discuss their views of the characters. Share ideas. Read the second extract of the story from the CD-ROM, either independently or as a class. Ask children to think again, with their partner, about their views of the main character and then share ideas as a class. **Plenary** Draw an emotion graph of the story. Use the boy's feelings towards the events to construct the graph.	**Extend:** write a reading journal entry about one of the characters, stating the views about him using evidence from the text
Empathy: other people's emotions		

DAY 3 ■ Character hot-seating

Key features	Stages	Additional opportunities
	Introduction Re-read the story *Hajj*, focusing on the characters. Discuss what we have learned about them: the main character/narrator, Gary, Robbie, Evelyn Levy, the narrator's father. What do we know about the relationships between them? Collect evidence about each character either by highlighting the text (a different colour for each character) or making posters for each one, inviting the children to add phrases/sentences from the text that tell us something about them.	
Empathy: causes of other people's emotions	**Speaking and listening** In pairs, ask children to prepare questions for all of the characters. Prompt the children to ask the characters why they act in the way they do, how they feel about situations in the story or events in the past, what they would like to be different. Hot-seat some children in the roles of the characters.	**Extend:** children hot-seat each other
	Plenary Draw an emotion graph for one of the other characters in the story (for example, Evelyn Levy), asking the children to imagine how life was for him before the war, during Dunkirk, after the war.	

DAY 4 ■ Handling time

Key features	Stages	Additional opportunities
	Introduction Prompt the children to identify that some of the story is written in the past tense and some in the present tense, and that the author is using the technique of flashback. Analyse the text to see how the author demonstrates the passing of time. You could highlight the time connectives in the story and the shifts between past and present tense verbs. Draw a graph or timeline to show the time structure of the story, noting how this is demonstrated.	
	Independent work Give the children paragraphs from the story and ask them to change them from past to present tense, or vice versa. Remind them that they may need to add or delete words or change the word order so that the paragraph makes sense. Some children could write a short passage of their own which includes shifts between the past and present tense.	**Extend:** ask children to write a passage from the point of view of one of the boys or Evelyn Levy
Reasoning: making deductions from text	**Plenary** Discuss the effect of using flashback. Does it add to the mood of the story? What is the impact of writing the story in the first person? How would the story be different if it were written from the point of view of one of the other boys?	

DAY 5 ■ Story themes

Key features	Stages	Additional opportunities
	## Introduction	
Reasoning: authorial intent	Ask children to reflect on the story *Hajj*. Ask them to consider the themes of the story, and generate a list. These may include relationships between generations, loss, trauma, misunderstanding, reconciliation, forgiveness, war. What did they like/dislike about the story? What do they think the author's message was? Was there a message or is it just a story?	
Evaluation: justify views and opinions	## Independent work
Ask children to write a review of the story commenting on the themes, what they like about the story and how the author structures the story. Give choices of how the children could present their review. Some may need a writing frame with subheadings. For example: *Themes, Story, Main relationships, Story structure...*	**Extend:** encourage children to comment on the language features in the text
	## Plenary
Invite the children to read their reviews to the class. The reviews could be made into a display or a class book.	

Guided reading
Read other short stories with a war theme, for example from *War Stories of Conflict* by Michael Morpurgo.

Assessment
Can the children comment on the mood of a story?
Can the children identify how the author indicates the passing of time? Refer back to the learning outcomes on page 57.

Further work
Make a list of time connectives, phrases that indicate the passing of time, phrases that indicate a flashback.
Use reading journal ideas to reflect on the story.

DAY 1 ■ Planning a narrative

Creative thinking: generate ideas in response to a piece of music

Introduction
Explain to the children that they are going to plan a narrative piece, based on the story *Hajj*, from the viewpoint of the narrator. Listen to a piece of music such as *Aquarium* by Saint Saens; discuss the mood of the music. Discuss how the story could be structured to fit the structure of the music.

Independent work
Allow the children to devise their own paragraph planner covering the key events in the story, or provide the photocopiable version (see photocopiable page 66 'Paragraph planner'). The children should consider eight paragraphs covering:
■ The recurring dream
■ Visiting the canal
■ Flashback to the boys teasing the old man
■ Flashback to the boys boarding *Virginia*
■ Flashback to untying boat/drowning
■ Boys swearing to keep the secret
■ Newspaper report 'War hero drowns'
■ Narrator's plan to join the army.
Ask them to make notes of ideas for each paragraph.

Plenary
Discuss and share the children's ideas, recording their suggestions on the board.

Support: draw sketches of the events for each paragraph and label them

Extend: tell the story from Gary/Robbie's viewpoint

DAY 2 ■ Paragraph planners

Creative thinking: generate ideas for a short narrative in response to a piece of music

Introduction
Model how to organise the memories and events into a linked sequence (this could be chronological or use shifts in time). Model mapping the paragraphs to phases in the music. You will need to listen to the music with the class and agree which phrases of the music will fit with each paragraph. Explain to the children that the plan will also form the basis of a visual ICT presentation and they need to note visual effects on their plan. You will need to establish the limitations depending on your ICT resources. Discuss how to indicate flashback – for example, by the use of conditionals, or through a visual technique such as colour.

Independent work
Ask the children to complete their paragraph plans, linking paragraphs to phases in the music. Remind the children that the narrative is to be written from the narrator's point of view. Ideas need to be noted as visual effects as well as written equivalents. This could be done using headphones on the computer to enable the children to listen repeatedly to the music. (If the facility for the children to listen to the music individually is not available, you could decide as a class which phrase of the music will fit which paragraph.)

Plenary
Share ideas and review plans. How are the children planning to convey mood, flashback and narrative viewpoint?

DAY 3 ■ Sentence surgery

Key features	Stages	Additional opportunities
Creative thinking: generate ideas in response to a piece of music	**Introduction** Using the paragraph planner, decide how many sentences each paragraph will need in order to convey the ideas and fit the time constraints of the music. Model writing the first paragraph of the narrative from the planner, indicating the passing of time and the mood of the memory. Model the use of tense, time conditionals, complex sentences and concise language. Once written, read the paragraph through to the musical phrase assigned to it, checking that it fits.	
Evaluation: give feedback to others	**Independent work** Children should begin their own narrative independently. They should be reminded to use time conditionals, phrases that convey mood and precise language to tell the story. Use response partners to offer feedback on the effectiveness of the sentences written.	**Extend:** if preferred, children could write extended paragraphs to retell the story rather than short precise ones
	Plenary Ask children to look at their sentences alongside their paragraph planner and identify a sentence they are having difficulty with to bring to a 'sentence surgery' in the next lesson – for example, a sentence where they have not been able to capture all the important aspects of the scene or have not been able to convey the mood.	**Support:** some children may write one sentence per scene

DAY 4 ■ Sentence surgery (2)

Key features	Stages	Additional opportunities
Evaluation: discuss success criteria	**Introduction** As a class, look at the sentences brought by the children to the 'sentence surgery'. Support the children to improve their sentences to ensure maximum impact on the reader, encourage other children to offer advice. Continue to use shared and supported composition to transfer the ideas from the planner into a narrative, make reference to the music to ensure the sections fit appropriately. With the children, create a checklist of features needed for the stories.	**Support:** use photocopiable page 67 'Sentence surgery'
Evaluation: give feedback to others	**Independent work** Children should continue to write their narratives independently, using response partners to offer feedback on their use of sentences. They should be reminded to use time conditionals, phrases that convey mood and precise language to tell the story.	**Support:** write their narratives in pairs
Evaluation: judge effectiveness of own work	**Plenary** Ask the children to self-evaluate their stories against the checklist of features agreed at the start of the lesson. Are they conveying mood, indicating time shifts, selecting precise language?	

DAY 5 ■ Flashback and mood

Key features	Stages	Additional opportunities
	### Introduction Go through the checklist of features with the children. Discuss any problems they may have with their narratives. Share ideas on how to convey shifts in time, collect effective vocabulary and phrases which convey mood and recap on the use of complex sentences. If appropriate, use this session to continue modelling writing based on the planner.	
	### Independent work Allow an extended writing session for the children to complete their narratives, providing support as necessary. Allow time for the children to read each others' narratives.	**Extend:** present their narratives as word-processed books
Evaluation: discuss success criteria; give feedback to others	### Plenary Provide time for peer evaluation of finished narratives against checklist of features. Compare the narratives written with the original story.	

DAY 6 ■ Visual story planning

Key features	Stages	Additional opportunities
Reasoning: discuss a short narrative film	### Introduction Tell the children they are going to make a visual version of the story. If possible, watch a short film (for example, *The Piano* by Aidan Gibbons) to examine visual techniques such as camera angle, colour, background and use of music. Discuss the film-maker's intent when making these choices. Ask the children what kind of images would be effective for their short story.	
Information processing: explore information communicated through different modes and use this to create own narrative	### Independent work With a partner, ask the children to select the key moment in each paragraph of their short story. Discuss the images they could use to represent each paragraph and how they can show the shift in time. Encourage the use of simple backgrounds and images as these will be easier to translate onto ICT-based presentations. Encourage them to create a pictorial storyboard of events using rough sketches to represent their ideas, using photocopiable page 68 'Visual storyboard' or making their own.	**ICT:** children may draw or paint images for use in their presentations in art; they could also use ICT-based art packages for their images
	### Plenary Invite children to share their ideas with the class, explaining their choice of image for each part of the story.	

DAY 7 ■ Images and mood

Key features	Stages	Additional opportunities
	Introduction Using one of the children's visual storyboards as a prompt, discuss how the images could be created for inserting into presentation software – drawings, artwork, photographs, moving pictures. Establish how the passing of time can be shown for example by changing the background.	
Information processing: create own narrative	**Independent work** In pairs, children should work on creating images to match their storyboard (see list above), to be scanned into the computer or downloaded from camera into a presentation. Remind children of the mood of the story and the need for simplistic images and images which are appropriate to the story, such as boats, canal, wartime images. They may wish to use the same image more than once.	**Support:** you may wish to supply a selection of appropriate images for the children to select from, such as photographs from the internet, (copyright permitting) wartime images
Evaluation: give feedback to others	**Plenary** Ask pairs to evaluate each other's images. Do they show the passing of time, convey the mood, and so on?	

DAY 8 ■ Slideshow stories

Key features	Stages	Additional opportunities
Evaluation: discuss success criteria	**Introduction** Model using presentation software ready prepared with slides containing images appropriate to the story. Show the children how to order the images and set the time for each image to the appropriate length of time indicated by the musical phrases. Demonstrate using tools such as fades and other transition effects. With the children, create success criteria for the short films. These might include images and musical phrases appropriately matched, images convey the mood effectively, images are simplistic and have impact.	
Creative thinking: a short narrative in response to music	**Independent work** Children should work on their own presentations, ensuring that the slideshow is set up to fit with the music. Ensure they are aware of the criteria by which they will be evaluated.	**Support:** create the slideshow independently of the music
Evaluation: judge effectiveness of own work	**Plenary** Ask children to self-assess their work against the criteria agreed. Use 'three stars and a wish' – three things they think they have done well and one which they would like to improve.	

DAY 9 ■ Film festival

Key features	Stages	Additional opportunities
Evaluation: give feedback to others	**Introduction** Invite children to show their films to response partners. Ask response partners to feedback on how effectively the narrative conveyed the mood and indicated the shifts between past and present, what they liked about it and any improvements they could suggest or ambiguities which need to be addressed.	
Evaluation: discuss success criteria	**Plenary** Show the short films to the rest of the class. Evaluate the films using the agreed criteria. What were the difficulties in making the films? What do they think has been successful? What are the benefits of a visual narrative over a written one? Invite other children, staff and parents to a 'Film Festival'. Display the written narratives, plans, storyboards and images alongside the film show to show the work undertaken to create the films.	**Extend:** if time allows, children could carry out improvements before the Film Festival

Guided reading
Read short stories from *War Stories of Conflict* edited by Michael Morpurgo.

Assessment
Can children use accurate sentence and paragraph construction?
Can children use a range of written and visual techniques to indicate shifts in time?
Can children use a range of written and visual techniques to create the mood of a narrative?
Ask the children to complete the CD-ROM assessment activity 'What's the mood?'
Refer back to the learning outcomes on page 57.

Further work
This Unit could be taught using the short film *The Piano* by Aidan Gibbons to inspire the narrative.
If the ICT software is not available, children could create artwork to accompany music.

Paragraph planner

■ Write your own paragraph planner covering the key points in the story, making notes for each paragraph. Write a short summary title for each paragraph.

Paragraph 1 _____	Paragraph 2 _____
Paragraph 3 _____	Paragraph 4 _____
Paragraph 5 _____	Paragraph 6 _____
Paragraph 7 _____	Paragraph 8 _____

100 LITERACY FRAMEWORK LESSONS YEAR 6

Name _____ **Date** _____

Sentence surgery

■ Use these time connectives and at least two clauses from the list to construct complex sentences:

For example: *Thinking back to times gone by, she wondered if she should have left, they had always been good to her.*

Time connectives

Thinking back to times gone by	By lunchtime	As long as she could remember
By this time	Suddenly	Many years ago
Haunted by events the day before	It had been too long	Back then
That moment	Previously	Later that day
Some time later	When he was younger	
	A few hours later	

Clauses

among the hills	towering above the tall trees	hesitating at the gate
it had been different		they had always been good to her
the church steeple had stood proud	as she skipped joyfully down the street	a football came flying over
he realised he never wanted to go to the park again	she wondered if she should have left	he hoped they'd go again
I took a deep breath	he loved it there	he recounted the events to his Dad
she hoped she would be able to visit Granny again soon	striking the post	he no longer had any enthusiasm
	their manes glinting in the bright June sun	
as fit as a fiddle	the children walked silently down their road	the horses were galloping across the hills
I had no choice	no one dared speak	

■ Compare your sentences with a partner. Could you improve them?

■ Now try writing your own complex sentences showing the passing of time.

Visual storyboard

■ Create a storyboard of events, making sketches in the boxes below to represent your ideas. In each box write a brief description of what is happening.

1	2
3	4
5	6
7	8

NON-FICTION
UNIT 1 Biography and autobiography

Speak and listen for a range of purposes on paper and on screen

Strand 1 Speaking
- Use the techniques of dialogic talk to explore ideas, topics or issues.

Strand 2 Listening and responding
- Make notes when listening for a sustained period and discuss how note-taking varies depending on context and purpose.

Strand 4 Drama
- Devise a performance considering how to adapt the performance for a specific audience.

Read for a range of purposes on paper and on screen

Strand 6 Word structure and spelling
- Spell familiar words correctly and employ a range of strategies to spell difficult and unfamiliar words.
- Use a range of appropriate strategies to edit, proofread and correct spelling in their own work, on paper and on screen.

Strand 7 Understanding and interpreting texts
- Appraise a text quickly, deciding on its value, quality or usefulness.
- Understand underlying themes, causes and points of view.

Strand 8 Engaging with and responding to texts
- Sustain engagement with longer texts, using different techniques to make the text come alive.
- Compare how writers from different times and places present experiences and use language.

Write for a range of purposes on paper and on screen

Strand 9 Creating and shaping texts
- Set their own challenges to extend achievement and experience in writing.
- Use different narrative techniques to engage and entertain the reader.
- Select words and language drawing on their knowledge of literary features and formal and informal writing.
- Integrate words, images and sounds imaginatively for different purposes.

Strand 10 Text structure and organisation
- Use varied structures to shape and organise text coherently.
- Use paragraphs to achieve pace and emphasis.

Strand 11 Sentence structure and punctuation
- Express subtle distinctions of meaning, including hypothesis, speculation and supposition, by constructing sentences in varied ways.

Strand 12 Presentation
- Select from a wide range of ICT programs to present text effectively and communicate information and ideas.

Progression in recounts

In this year children are moving towards:
- Distinguishing between biography and autobiography, recognising the effect on the reader of the choice between first and third person, distinguishing between fact, opinion and fiction, and between implicit and explicit points of view and how these can differ.

UNIT 1 ◄ Biography and autobiography *continued*

- Developing the skills of biographical and autobiographical writing in role, composing a biographical account based on research.
- Selecting the appropriate style and form to suit a specific purpose and audience, when planning writing, drawing on knowledge of different text types.

Key aspects of learning covered in this Unit

Enquiry
Children will identify their own key questions about a particular life, and then locate the evidence to answer it within a range of sources.

Information processing
Children will identify relevant information from a range of sources on paper and on screen and use this as a basis for both oral presentation and writing.

Evaluation
Children will present information orally and in writing. They will discuss success criteria, give feedback to others and judge the effectiveness of their own work.

Reasoning
Children will construct reasoned arguments based on available information and evidence.

Empathy
Through discussing and writing simulated autobiography, children will need to imagine themselves in another person's position.

Communication
Children will develop their ability to discuss and debate issues in respect of both the form and the content of the biographical texts they are reading and writing. They will communicate outcomes orally, in writing and through using other modes and media.

Prior learning

Before starting this Unit check that the children can:
- Identify and discuss: the language and organisational features of texts; elements of persuasion in texts; the comparative advantages of using words, images and sounds when communicating through multimodal text.
- Understand how texts can be adapted to suit different purposes/audiences.
If they need further support please refer to a prior Unit or a similar Unit in Year 5.

Resources

Phase 1:
Books by Malorie Blackman; Photocopiable page 83 'My autobiography'; *Malorie Blackman Biography* ✅; Photocopiable page 84 'Recount checklist'; Other biographical information about Malorie Blackman; Internet access
Phase 2:
Presentation resources – such as computer software and music
Phase 3:
Malorie Blackman Biography ✅; Photocopiable page 84 'Recount checklist'; Internet access
Phase 4:
Photocopiable page 85 'KWL grid'; *Malorie Blackman Biography* ✅; Photocopiable page 86 'Planning a biography'; Assessment activity 'True or false?'

Cross-curricular opportunities

Biographical writing about people in other curricular areas (history, science, art)

UNIT 1 ■ Teaching sequence

Phase	Children's objectives	Summary of activities	Learning outcomes
1	I can find information about an author.	Reading and note making.	Children can extract and interpret key information. Children can evaluate the reliability and usefulness of information. Children can understand the terms 'biography' and 'autobiography'.
2	I can develop questions for research. I can prepare and give an effective presentation.	Reading and note making. Developing oral presentations. Giving and evaluating presentations.	Children can research, prepare and present orally an account of a life.
3	I can analyse a biography and autobiography.	Identifying structural and linguistic features.	Children can recognise the structure and language, and organisational features of different forms of biography and autobiography.
4	I can turn a biography into an autobiography. I can identify key information. I can give an oral biography. I can plan, write and present a biography.	Planning and writing. Reading and note making. Speaking and listening. Making presentations.	Children can write an effective biography selecting language, form, format and content to suit a particular audience and purpose.

Provide copies of the objectives for the children.

DAY 1 ▪ Introducing biography and autobiography

Key features	Stages	Additional opportunities
	### Introduction Explain to the children that in this Unit they will be exploring biographies and autobiographies. Ask whether they know what these two texts are and how they differ. Agree on and write up a definition for each. Show the children a number of books by Malorie Blackman and explain that they will be reading about and researching her life. Ask whether they have read any of the books that you are showing them. What do they know about Malorie Blackman herself? Record any responses on a *Malorie Blackman fact sheet* in a format that the children can add to as they progress through the Unit.	
Communication: relay information coherently	### Speaking and listening Ask the children to work in pairs and to spend five minutes each telling their partner about their lives. Once the activity has been completed, ask: *How were the retellings organised? What tense did the speakers use? Did you find out anything that you didn't previously know?*	**Support:** give children prompts to structure their retelling (see photocopiable page 83 'My autobiography')
Information processing: identify relevant information	### Independent work Give out copies of the books by Malorie Blackman to small groups of children. Ask them to look carefully at the books and to note down any information they can find about the author. You may wish to model how it is possible to make inferences and deductions from information.	
	### Plenary Take feedback from the activity and add the information the children found to the *Malorie Blackman fact sheet.*	

DAY 2 ▪ Identifying key information

Key features	Stages	Additional opportunities
Information processing: identify key events **Information processing:** record key events	### Introduction Explain to the children that they are going to read a biography of Malorie Blackman and identify key events in her life. Display the text from the CD-ROM. Ask the children to read it through once to themselves, mentally noting the key events. Read it through as a class, highlighting the key events identified by the children. Discuss how the key events could be recorded in a way that shows chronology (for example, as a timeline). You may wish to use photocopiable page 84 'Recount checklist' for this purpose.	**Support:** provide a timeline with some key events already recorded for children to add to
	### Independent work Ask the children to record the key events in a format that they feel is suitable.	
Reasoning: support opinion by referring to text	### Plenary Invite some children to explain the format they have chosen and why they chose it. Revisit the biography. Ask the children whether there is any additional information that isn't a key event but they find interesting. Involve children in highlighting this. Add it to the fact sheet started in the previous lesson. Discuss with the children who they think the biography was written for (audience) and why (purpose). Encourage them to justify their responses by referring to the text for evidence.	

DAY 3 ■ Identifying key information

Key features	Stages	Additional opportunities
	Introduction Remind the children of the biography they read in the previous lesson. Explain that they are now going to see other texts that contain some biographical information about Malorie Blackman. Before the lesson source some material about Malorie Blackman, ideally a newspaper interview (copyright permitting). Show this to the children and ask them to read it through and consider the purpose and audience.	**Extend:** children can look in books by Malorie Blackman for references to websites and other sources of information
Information processing: identify key information	**Independent work** Encourage the children to read through the text and to note down any new information that they find. They can add any new key events to those they recorded in the previous lesson.	
Communication: collaborate as a group	**Speaking and listening** Ask the children to work in small groups and to share their notes. Each group should allocate a spokesperson to feed back to the class. Ask them also to consider whether there was anything in the interview that they liked or disliked, and whether they noticed any puzzles or patterns.	
	Plenary Take feedback from the group discussions. Record any additional interesting information on the fact sheet. Discuss any likes, dislikes, puzzles or patterns noticed by the children. Explore the similarities and differences between the two biographical texts that they have read so far.	

DAY 4 ■ Exploring autobiography

Key features	Stages	Additional opportunities
	Introduction Remind the children that they have looked at a biography of Malorie Blackman. Explain that they are now going to explore some autobiographical writing. Focus on the word *autobiography*. Explain that the prefix *auto* comes from the Greek word *autos*, meaning *self*.	**Extend:** ask children to find examples of other words with the prefix *auto*
Information processing: identify and record key information	**Independent work** Allow children time to explore Malorie Blackman's website (www.malorieblackman.co.uk) and to note down any new information that they find. Ask them to consider how reading information written by Malorie Blackman herself is different from reading information written by someone else.	
Communication: discuss the form and content of biography and autobiography	**Plenary** Ask the children where they found the information on the website. Discuss how Malorie Blackman gives information about herself on virtually every page on the website – not just on the biography page. Add any extra new information to the fact sheet that you started in the first lesson. What do the children find most interesting about the author? Discuss the validity of information found in biographies and autobiographies. Explore with the children how knowing the source of the information might affect their view of the subject and their acceptance, or not, of the truth of the information. Which source of information do the children feel has been the most useful and informative? Discuss the reasons behind their responses. Can any further facts be added to the fact sheet?	

Guided reading

Malorie Blackman has written books for children with a range of reading abilities. It should be possible to identify an appropriate title for most children to read in guided reading sessions.

Are the children able to identify any aspects of the books that appear to have been influenced by Malorie Blackman's life and experiences?

Assessment

Identify and record key information (teacher observation, self-assessment).

Appraise a text for its usefulness and validity (teacher observation, self-assessment).

Refer back to the learning outcomes on page 71.

Further work

Support children in using skimming and scanning skills to look for key words and phrases.

Encourage children to be critical readers and to use organisational devices (such as contents, index) to establish whether a text will give the information they are looking for.

DAY 1 ■ Developing questions for research

Key features	Stages	Additional opportunities
	Introduction Revisit the Malorie Blackman fact sheet developed during previous lessons. Remind the children how much they now know about the author. Discuss what impact they feel her life and experiences might have had on her writing. Explain that this is an area that they are going to research. Rephrase it as a question and record it for the children to refer to during their research.	
Enquiry: formulate questions	**Speaking and listening** Ask children, in small groups, to discuss what further information they would like to find out about Malorie Blackman. They should record this as a series of questions and establish how they propose to carry out this research.	
Enquiry: research answers	**Independent work** Allow children time to research both their own questions and that discussed earlier as a class. Remind them to record the source of information, particularly if using the internet, as well as recording the information itself.	**Support:** work in mixed-ability groups **Extend:** record sources of information using the conventions of a bibliography
	Plenary Discuss the children's research. Focus particularly on any evidence the children have that Malorie Blackman's life and experiences have had an impact on her writing. Explore the sources of the information. Do the children feel it is valid? How can they check?	

DAY 2 ■ Preparing a presentation

Key features	Stages	Additional opportunities
	Introduction Remind the children that they now know a huge amount of information about Malorie Blackman. Explain that, in their research groups, they are going to develop and prepare a short oral presentation about the author to the rest of the class. You may wish to set a time limit of five minutes for each presentation. Discuss the different forms of visual support that the children could use during their presentations such as interactive whiteboard and presentation software. Establish that they should focus on the research question formulated in the previous lesson: what impact has Malorie Blackman's life and experiences had on her writing?	
Information processing: use research as the basis for a presentation	**Independent work** Allow the groups time to plan and prepare their presentations. Encourage the creative use of ICT, for example using music to enhance aspects of the presentation. Ensure that each group member is clear about the role they will play during the presentation.	**Support:** work in mixed-ability groups
	Plenary Discuss the progress of each group, asking a spokesperson to report to the class on any particular problems and successes that they have had. As a class, establish some ground rules for the presentations – for both speakers and listeners. You may wish to record and display these.	

DAY 3 ■ Giving and evaluating presentations

Key features	Stages	Additional opportunities
	Introduction Explain to the children that before they start making their presentations, they need to establish some success criteria against which the presentations can be evaluated.	
Evaluation: discuss success criteria	**Speaking and listening** Allow children time in their groups to discuss possible success criteria. Take feedback from the discussions and, as a class, decide on three or four criteria. Record and display these.	
Communication: make presentations	**Independent work** Remind the children of the ground rules developed in the previous lesson. Ask each group to present their presentations. Remind the rest of the class to listen carefully, allowing time after each presentation for them to discuss and evaluate it against the success criteria.	**Support:** children can work in mixed-ability groups
Evaluation: give and receive feedback	**Plenary** Suggest to the groups that when they feedback on the presentations, they could adopt a 'good news sandwich' structure: start and finish with positive points, if there is a criticism, it can be sandwiched between the good news. Remind the children that if they are going to make criticisms about a presentation, they must be prepared to suggest how it could be improved. Allow time for feedback, facilitating discussion about the quality of both the content and the presentation styles.	

Guided reading

Use non-fiction texts during guided reading to support children's acquisition of skimming and scanning skills.
Ask them to find specific information in a text quickly and efficiently, encouraging the use of organisational devices such as contents and index.

Assessment

Present in an interesting and articulate manner (feedback from other children, teacher observation).
Support points of view with evidence (feedback from other children, teacher observation).
Refer back to the learning outcomes on page 71.

Further work

Support children's communication and presentation skills through the use and analysis of video and audio recordings. Model and demonstrate how to make a statement, then support it with evidence. This can be both orally and in writing.

DAY 1 ▪ Analysing biographies

Key features	Stages	Additional opportunities
Enquiry: analyse structure of a text	### Introduction Return to the biography of Malorie Blackman from the CD-ROM. Ask the children to remind you of the purpose of a biography, for example to give information about a person's life. Remind the children that this is a non-fiction text. Ask them to read through it to identify how the information is organised (chronologically). Through discussion, lead the children to understand that a biography is a recount. It may be helpful to talk about recounts as a family of text types – a biography is a member of that family. Explore the use of paragraphs to group events from a similar time frame together.	
Enquiry: analyse language features	### Independent work Print copies of the biography from the CD-ROM. In pairs, children can explore the biography, identifying and highlighting the language features that indicate it is part of the recount family (for example, the use of dates, past tense).	**Support:** provide children with a checklist of language features of recounts (photocopiable page 84)
	### Plenary Display the biography from the CD-ROM. Take feedback from the activity, highlighting the language features that the children have identified. Focus on the use of the third person, ensuring that children understand that this is a key indicator of a biography. Point out the shifts between past and present tense and why the tense changes. Develop a list of the organisational and linguistic features of a biography. Display this for children to refer to during the rest of the Unit.	

DAY 2 ▪ Analysing biography and autobiography

Key features	Stages	Additional opportunities
Enquiry: identify facts and opinions	### Introduction Remind the children of the analysis activities they did in the previous lesson, referring to the list of features that was developed. Return to the biography from the CD-ROM. Explain that, together, you are going to look for facts and opinions in the text. Highlight these, using one colour for the facts and another for the opinions. Discuss the difference between the two. Focus the children's attention on the use of quotes to add credibility.	
	### Speaking and listening In pairs, children can take it in turns to state a fact and to give an opinion.	
Enquiry: analyse structure and language features of a text	### Independent work Display the biography page on Malorie Blackman's website (www.malorieblackman.co.uk). Ask the children, in pairs, to identify how it is organised and how the language features compare to those of a biography. Are they able to identify the facts and opinions in the text?	**Extend:** provide other examples of biographies and autobiographies, allowing children time to explore the manipulation of chronology
	### Plenary Discuss the children's responses to the activity. Explore the use of chronology in the text and how Malorie Blackman has moved from writing about one period in her life back to an earlier period. Ask the children why they think she has organised the text in this way. Establish that both biographies and autobiographies can be organised like this. Have children noticed the use of the first person? Establish that this is a key indicator of an autobiography.	

Guided reading

During guided reading, provide examples of biographies and autobiographies. Ask children to identify facts and opinions. Encourage them to become critical readers, questioning facts and opinions as they read.

Assessment

Identify the structure and language features of biographies and autobiographies (teacher observation). Refer back to the learning outcomes on page 71.

Further work

Give children opportunities to explore and compare other examples of biographies and autobiographies. Establish that information can be presented in a number of formats but it remains essentially chronological.

DAY 1 ◼ Turning biography into autobiography

Key features	Stages	Additional opportunities
Evaluation: develop success criteria **Communication:** hot-seating **Empathy:** think of another person's position **Information processing:** use researched information **Evaluation:** judge effectiveness of writing	**Introduction** As a class, discuss the children's knowledge and understanding of biographies and autobiographies and the similarities and differences between them. Explain that in this lesson, they are going to use the information they have collected over the past two weeks to write an autobiographical text, as if they were Malorie Blackman. Together, develop a list of two or three success criteria that will be used to evaluate the children's writing. **Speaking and listening** In groups, children can share what they know about the author through hot-seating, where one takes the role of Malorie Blackman and the rest of the group ask her questions. **Independent work** Working individually, children can plan and write their Malorie Blackman autobiographies. **Plenary** Ask some children to read their autobiographies. Encourage the rest of the class to refer to the success criteria developed earlier in the lesson in order to evaluate the pieces of writing.	**Support:** ensure children understand the need to write consistently in the first person

DAY 2 ◼ Researching information

Key features	Stages	Additional opportunities
	Introduction Explain to the children that, over the next few lessons, they are going to be planning and writing biographies of a person of their choice. This could be anyone from a favourite sports personality to a member of their family. Ensure, however, that they understand the reality of this and don't choose a subject who will be difficult to research. The culmination of this work will be a ceremony where the children are introducing their chosen subject by reading their biographies to the audience. Remind the children that they need to formulate some questions in order to carry out their research.	
Enquiry: formulate questions and find information	**Independent work** Allow the children both time and resources to research their chosen subject. Ensure that they are clear on how to make and keep notes and record the sources of their information. **Plenary** Ask some children to report back on progress so far, any problems they have encountered and useful tips for the rest of the class.	**Support:** provide a KWL grid for the children to structure their research (see photocopiable page 85)

DAY 3 ◼ Oral recounts

Key features	Stages	Additional opportunities
Evaluation: develop success criteria	**Introduction** Review the children's progress. Tell them that in order to 'limber up' for the writing activity, as they would before exercising, they are going to tell biographies orally. Together, develop two or three success criteria that can be used to evaluate the oral biographies. Choose a member of your own family as the subject of your oral biography and model telling the children about that person's life.	
Information processing: use research as basis for oral presentation	**Independent work** Allow children time to gather their facts together in order to prepare for the oral biography activity.	
Evaluation: judge effectiveness of oral presentation	**Speaking and listening** Children can work in small groups, telling their oral biographies. Encourage the rest of the group to give feedback after each child has had a turn, using the agreed success criteria.	**Support:** children can work in mixed-ability groups
	Plenary Take general feedback on the oral biography activity. Was there anything that the children found particularly challenging or would do differently next time?	

DAY 4 ◼ Planning a biography

Key features	Stages	Additional opportunities
Enquiry: analyse structure	**Introduction** Remind the children that they are going to be introducing the subject of their biographies at a ceremony and this is the reason for researching and writing about their lives. If appropriate, show the children footage of an award ceremony where the winners are introduced with a brief biography. It may be necessary to remind children to include a section on achievements in the biographies. Return to the Malorie Blackman biography from the CD-ROM. Explain to the children that together they are going to look again at how it is organised but this time focusing on the function and content of each paragraph. Read each paragraph and discuss how you could give a heading to it in order to summarise the content. For example: paragraph 1 – who and when; paragraph 2 – work; paragraph 3 – writing and achievements. Explain to the children that they can use these headings (or similar) to plan their biographies. You may wish to model this using a member of your family as the subject.	**Support:** provide children with a writing frame (see photocopiable page 86 'Planning a biography')
Information processing: plan biographies	**Independent work** Children can plan their biographies using the material they have researched on their chosen subject.	
	Plenary Discuss the children's progress.	

DAY 5 ■ Writing a biography

Key features	Stages	Additional opportunities
Communication: discuss formats	**Introduction** Tell the children that in this lesson they will be writing their biographies. As a class, discuss the various formats that these could take (for example, paper-based, IT-based). Remind them that they are introducing their subject at a ceremony so some visuals would be useful.	
	Speaking and listening Ask children in pairs or small groups to discuss formats for their own individual biographies. Encourage them to respond to ideas and make suggestions.	
Information processing: write biographies	**Independent work** Allow time for children to write the biographies and to bring them to an appropriate standard for presentation.	**Support:** provide children with a writing frame (see photocopiable page 86)
Evaluation: develop success criteria	**Plenary** Agree a format for the presentation ceremony with the children. If appropriate, allocate roles to some children (for example, Master/Mistress of Ceremonies) and invite a wider audience than just the class. Agree upon two or three success criteria on which to evaluate the presentations. List these and display them for use during and after the ceremony.	

DAY 6 ■ Presenting biographies

Key features	Stages	Additional opportunities
	Introduction Remind the children of the agreed format for the presentation ceremony. If necessary, allow them time to rehearse their presentations.	
Communication: effective presentations	**Speaking and listening** Carry out the ceremony as planned.	
Evaluation: review presentations	**Plenary** Review the success of the ceremony. Ask the children to evaluate first their own presentation, then that of a friend. Together recap on the children's knowledge of biographies and autobiographies. Discuss when they might write biographies in other curricular areas (such as history, art or science) and how they could use what they have learned during this Unit.	

Guided reading

In guided writing, support children in structuring their biographies in terms of chronology and paragraphing.
Examine in detail the variety of sentence structures in the biography of Malorie Blackman on the CD-ROM. Involve the children in changing word order in sentences and the effect that this has.

Assessment

Write an effective biography for a particular audience and purpose (marking and feedback against agreed success criteria).
Ask the children to complete the CD-ROM assessment activity 'True or false?'.
Refer back to the learning outcomes on page 71.

Further work

Give children alternative audiences and explore how this affects the style and format of their biographies.

My autobiography

◼ Fill in the sections below, writing in as much detail as possible. Use it to help tell your partner all about yourself.

Name
Date and place of birth
Family and pets
A big event in your life (what it was, when it happened)
Hobbies and interests
What you are good at
What you would change about yourself
Your ambitions

NON-FICTION ■ UNIT 1

Recount checklist

■ These are the features that are usually found in recount texts. Tick the features that you can find in the text you are looking at and give examples of these features.

■ Recounts usually:

Are about a particular person or people. Who is this recount based on?	☐
Include details of when and where. Give examples:	☐
Are written in the past tense. Give examples:	☐
Use first person (I, we) or third person (he, she, they) pronouns. Give examples:	☐
Use words to do with time (for example, first, next). Give examples:	☐
Include dates. Give examples:	☐
Include facts and opinions. Give examples:	☐

■ 100 LITERACY FRAMEWORK LESSONS YEAR 6

KWL grid

What I know	What I would like to know	What I have learned

Name _____   Date _____

Planning a biography

■ Use the categories below to help you plan and write your biography.

Person's name
Date and place of birth
What they are known for
Early life (for example: school life, childhood, family, what they liked and disliked)
Working life (for example: what they do/did as a career, how they got there, their ambitions)
Achievements (for example: awards, prizes, recognition for something)
Interests and hobbies
What they do now
Rounding off statement (for example: interesting or unusual fact, why you admire the person)

100 LITERACY FRAMEWORK LESSONS YEAR 6

PHOTOCOPIABLE   ■ SCHOLASTIC
www.scholastic.co.uk

NON-FICTION
UNIT 2 Journalistic writing

Speak and listen for a range of purposes on paper and on screen

Strand 1 Speaking
- Use a range of oral techniques to present persuasive arguments.
- Use the techniques of dialogic talk to explore ideas, topics or issues.

Strand 2 Listening and responding
- Make notes when listening for a sustained period.

Strand 4 Drama
- Improvise using a range of drama strategies to explore themes.

Read for a range of purposes on paper and on screen

Strand 6 Word structure and spelling
- Spell familiar words correctly and employ a range of strategies to spell difficult and unfamiliar words.
- Use a range of appropriate strategies to edit, proofread and correct spelling in their own work, on paper and on screen.

Strand 7 Understanding and interpreting texts
- Appraise a text quickly, deciding on its value, quality or usefulness.
- Recognise rhetorical devices used to persuade, mislead and sway the reader.

Strand 8 Engaging with and responding to texts
- Sustain engagement with longer texts.
- Compare how writers from different times and places present experiences and use language.

Write for a range of purposes on paper and on screen

Strand 9 Creating and shaping texts
- Use different narrative techniques to engage and entertain the reader.
- Select words and language drawing on their knowledge of literary features and formal and informal writing.
- Integrate words, images and sounds imaginatively for different purpose.

Strand 10 Text structure and organisation
- Use varied structures to shape and organise texts coherently.

Strand 11 Sentence structure and punctuation
- Express subtle distinctions of meaning, including hypothesis, speculation and supposition, by constructing sentences in varied ways.

Strand 12 Presentation
- Select from a wide range of ICT programs to present text effectively and communicate information and ideas.

Progression in information texts

In this year children are moving towards:
- Constructing and following a plan for researching further information.
- Evaluating the status of source material, looking for possible bias and comparing different sources on the same subject.
- Evaluating the language, style and effectiveness of non-fiction writing.
- Writing information texts, selecting the appropriate style and form to suit a specific purpose and audience, drawing on knowledge of different text types.
- Establishing, balancing and maintaining viewpoints.
- Discussing and explaining differences in the use of formal language.

Key aspects of learning covered in this Unit

Enquiry
Children will learn to ask: *Who? What? Where? When?* and *Why?* in researching a news story for a written or oral report.

Information processing
Children will identify relevant information from a range of sources on paper and on screen and use this as a basis for both oral and written reporting.

Evaluation
Children will read, compare and evaluate news from a variety of sources. When presenting news reports orally and in writing, they will discuss success criteria, give feedback to others and judge the effectiveness of their own work.

Reasoning
Children will construct reasoned arguments based on available information and evidence.

Empathy
In discussing and writing about real or simulated events, children will need to imagine themselves in another person's situation.

Communication
Children will develop their ability to discuss and debate issues in respect of both the content and the presentation of the news reports they are reading and writing. They will often work collaboratively in pairs and groups. They will communicate outcomes orally (in the style of radio broadcasts), in writing and through using other modes and media.

Prior learning

Before starting this Unit check that the children can:
■ Identify and discuss the language and organisational features of information texts.
■ Use a range of questions to elicit relevant information.
■ Plan, research and write a non-fiction script.
■ Work with others to deliver a polished performance of a script and evaluate their own performance.
If they need further support please refer to a prior Unit or a similar Unit in Year 5.

Resources

Phase 1:
After the freeze come the floods from the *Cornish and Devon Post* ❦; Floods news item ❦; Photocopiable page 100 'Identifying information in news articles'; Two photographs of Boscastle floods ❦

Phase 2:
Internet access; A radio interview (copyright permitting); Photocopiable page 101 'Headlines'; TV interviews (copyright permitting)

Phase 3:
Photocopiable page 101 'Headlines'

Phase 4:
Photocopiable page 102 'News report writing frame'; Assessment activity 'Journalistic writing evaluation' ❦

Cross-curricular opportunities

History

UNIT 2 ■ Teaching sequence

Phase	Children's objectives	Summary of activities	Learning outcomes
1	I can find information to answer questions I can make notes while watching broadcast. I can compare news reports.	Reading and text marking. Watching TV broadcast and note making. Comparing texts.	Children can understand what is being communicated, why and how.
2	I can research to find information to answer questions. I can identify interview techniques. I can establish existing knowledge. I can identify and use open questions.	Researching using the internet. Exploring radio broadcasts. Identifying the focus for a news story. Exploring interviewing through role play. Using questions.	Children can listen attentively to a news broadcast. Children can understand some of the key features of a radio news programme. Children can use discussion and drama techniques to explore a situation and its participants.
3	I can identify the structure and language features of newspaper articles.	Analysing newspaper articles.	Children can recognise the structure and language features of news articles.
4	I can organise a newspaper article. I can establish a point of view. I can turn notes into continuous text. I can establish criteria for presentations. I can make and evaluate presentations.	Planning a news article. Planning and writing an article. Rehearsing and recording broadcasts.	Children can write and present an effective news broadcast.

Provide copies of the objectives for the children.

DAY 1 ■ Introducing journalistic writing

Key features	Stages	Additional opportunities
	Introduction Explain to the children that in this Unit they will be exploring journalistic writing. Ask what they understand by this. Where would they expect to see this type of writing? What might it be about? Establish that journalistic writing appears in texts such as newspapers, magazines, newsletters and leaflets and is about events and situations that are of interest to the public. Write the following words for the class: *Who? Where? When? What? Why?* Explain that a news report should contain some information about these questions.	
Enquiry: ask *who, where, when, what, why* questions when reading an article	**Independent work** Give the children the newspaper article, *After the freeze come the floods* from the CD-ROM. Ask them to read the article through with a partner and to try to identify information about the five questions listed earlier. You may wish to ask the children to use five different-coloured markers to highlight the information.	**Support:** provide adult support to help children identify the relevant information; use photocopiable page 100 'Identifying information in news articles'
Information processing: identify relevant information	**Plenary** Work through the article with the children, highlighting the relevant information as they feed back on their reading. Were any of the questions more difficult to answer than others? Focus on identifying who the article is about. Are the children able to explain why the flood happened? (For example, melting snow, torrential rainfall.)	

DAY 2 ■ Exploring news broadcasts

Key features	Stages	Additional opportunities
	Introduction Show the children a brief example of a TV news broadcast (copyright permitting), or show the one from the CD-ROM. Ask: *How do you think the broadcaster knows what to say?* Focus the discussion on the use of an autocue. Establish that the news is written by journalists and that TV news stories, like newspaper articles, should also contain information related to the five questions explored in the previous lesson. Tell the children that they are going to watch another TV news broadcast in order to identify this information. Discuss how they can make notes when watching a broadcast. Suggest that writing down the five question words, then making notes under the relevant heading, will support them in this task.	**ICT:** if you wish to focus on the same news story in this Unit, TV and radio news broadcasts (copyright permitting)about the floods in Boscastle in 2004 can be found online by typing 'Boscastle floods' into a search engine
Enquiry: ask *who, where, when, what, why* questions when watching a news broadcast	**Independent work** Ask the children to watch the video clip (with voice-over) on the CD-ROM. Encourage them to make notes, in pairs, as they watch. You may need to play the clip two or three times. Children could use photocopiable page 100 'Identifying information in news articles' to help them make notes.	
Evaluation: compare and evaluate news from a variety of sources	**Plenary** Take feedback from the activity. Did the children find out any information that the newspaper article had not told them? Are there any differences or similarities between the articles they have read and seen? Which did they find most informative and interesting? Encourage the children to back up their opinions by referring to the text (both written and spoken). Discuss with the children whether they found the TV news activity more challenging than the newspaper activity in the previous lesson. Did working in pairs help them?	

DAY 3 ■ Comparing news reports

Key features	Stages	Additional opportunities
Information processing: identify relevant information	**Introduction** Collect together a number of appropriate newspaper articles (ensure you have an NLA licence) about events that involve and refer to specific people. **Independent work** In pairs, ask the children to read one of the articles closely and to focus on the people who are referred to. They should list those directly involved in the event and how they are referred to, and those not directly involved (such as spokespersons) and how they are referred to.	
Evaluation: read, compare and evaluate news from a variety of sources	**Plenary** Take feedback from the paired activity. Explore differences between the articles and the way that people are referred to. Discuss information that is given that is not necessarily relevant or necessary – for example, the inclusion of people's ages. Draw the children's attention to the use of quotes and reported speech in the articles. Explore the types of information given in the quotes.	**Support:** show children how to use highlighting techniques to identify these features

Guided reading

Give children other appropriate newspaper articles and ask them to identify information that answers the questions: *Who? Where? When? What? Why?*

Assessment

Appraise news reports and assess the purpose and intended audience (teacher observation, self-assessment).
Analyse news reports in order to identify key information (teacher observation, self-assessment).
Refer back to the learning outcomes on page 89.

Further work

Support children in thinking about the information a news report is giving and the features that indicate the target audience.
Encourage children to use highlighting and other text-marking techniques to identify key information in a news report.

DAY 1 ■ Researching using the internet

Key features	Stages	Additional opportunities
	Introduction Remind the children that they have read and watched news reports about floods in Boscastle. Explain that in this lesson they are going to build up a bigger picture of the event in order to add to their knowledge and understanding of what happened.	
	Speaking and listening In small groups, children can discuss and list what they already know about the flood, based on what they have read and watched so far. Take feedback and list what the children have identified. Read through the list and discuss which are facts and which are opinions. Establish, through discussion, what else the children would like to find out about the event. Record these as questions. For example: *Where is Boscastle? What damage was done? What has happened since?*	
Information processing: identify relevant information from a range of sources	**Independent work** Give the children the opportunity to research the listed questions using the internet. Ask them to record the information that they find.	**Support:** help children to identify appropriate sources for their research
	Plenary Take feedback from the independent research activity. Were the children able to find answers to the questions? Explore how they went about finding websites to support their research. Have they discovered any discrepancies in the information?	

DAY 2 ■ Exploring radio broadcasts

Key features	Stages	Additional opportunities
	Introduction Discuss the children's findings about what happened to people who were in Boscastle on that day. What have they found out about how people were rescued?	
	Speaking and listening In pairs, ask children to discuss how it might have felt to be involved in the flood. In small groups, they can explore this further through role playing a rescue or hot-seating people involved in the rescue. Explain to the children that they are going to listen to a radio interview (copyright permitting) with someone who was involved in the floods and make notes about what they hear. Discuss effective note-making techniques, such as having a clear listening focus, noting down key words and information, not writing out the whole of the interview verbatim.	
Information processing: identify relevant information	**Independent work** In groups, ask children to listen to the radio interview. Each group should focus on one aspect of the interview, such as the questions the interviewer asks, the type of language used, the way the interviewer prompts the interviewee, how they think the interviewee felt during the interview.	
	Plenary Take feedback from the independent activity. Discuss the effectiveness of the notes that the children have made and how they can be improved.	

DAY 3 ▪ Identifying the focus for a news story

Key features	Stages	Additional opportunities
	Introduction Explain to the children that, in small groups, they are going to start working on developing their own news reports. As a class, explore events that could form the basis for their reports. This could be a real event, one that relates to another curriculum area, such as a historical event, an event in the class novel or an imaginary event. Ask each group, through discussion, to identify the event they are going to focus on.	**Support:** guide children in their choice of event, ensuring that they will have access to sufficient information
Communication: work collaboratively towards an agreed goal	**Independent work** Working in their groups, children can discuss and list what they know about the events under the five question words identified earlier in the Unit: *Who? Where? When? What? Why?*	
	Plenary Explore the groups' knowledge of their chosen events. If they need more information, discuss how they can go about researching the event or developing their ideas further. Explain that they will initially be writing a news report about their chosen event and then developing this into a radio broadcast. Discuss how, having read, watched and heard news reports, they can use their existing knowledge of news reports to help them in their writing. Ask the groups to identify an audience for their radio broadcasts. Remind them that they need to be aware of this audience as they write.	

DAY 4 ▪ Exploring interviewing through role play

Key features	Stages	Additional opportunities
	Introduction Remind the children that in the previous lesson, they identified an event that will be the focus for their own radio news broadcasts. Explain that in this lesson, they are going to concentrate on one of the main characters involved in the event. Revisit the work done on the Boscastle floods and how 'human interest' was at the centre of many, if not most, of the reports they have watched, read and listened to. Discuss why they think this is the case; for example, people are interested in hearing about other people's situations. You may wish to broaden this discussion to include matters of taste and decency and when it is right or wrong to report on people's misfortunes and tragedies.	
Empathy: discuss events by imagining another person's situation and feelings	**Speaking and listening** Working in their groups, children can identify one of the main characters. In threes, children should adopt the roles of interviewer, interviewee and observer. Through role play they can then explore an interview situation in which the interviewer questions the interviewee. The observer can note the questions asked and which were more effective than others in gaining information. It would be helpful to record the interviews.	**Support:** help children to develop suitable questions, encouraging them to use open rather than closed questions if necessary
	Plenary As a class, explore the observers' interpretations of the role plays. Focus on open questions and discuss with the children how this type of question encourages the interviewee to give longer and more detailed responses. If necessary, ask the children to write down some examples of open questions.	

DAY 5 ■ Using questions

Key features	Stages	Additional opportunities
	### Introduction Remind the children of the interviewing they did in the previous lesson and the questions they identified as being particularly effective. Explain that they are going to watch examples of TV interviews (ERA licence permitting) to see how professional interviewers use the open questioning technique. Ask them to draw up two columns on a sheet of paper headed *Open* and *Closed*. Ensure that children understand the difference between the two question types.	
Evaluation: evaluate interviewing and questioning techniques	### Independent work Give time for children to watch the interview through once and to record the number of open and closed questions asked by the interviewer. On subsequent viewings they can note down the wording in the open questions. Children can then compare the wording with the questions that they asked in the previous lesson. You may wish to use the recorded interviews here. Are they able to rephrase some of the closed questions so that they become open?	**Support:** use recorded examples of appropriate TV interviews for this activity
	### Plenary Ask the children whether the TV interviewer used more open or closed questions. Were they able to successfully reword some of their own closed questions? You may wish to ask them to try asking their reworded questions and consider whether they elicit a more effective response. Discuss with the children whether they noticed any other techniques the interviewer used, such as facial gestures to encourage a response, encouraging gestures or comments.	

Guided reading

Using information texts at an appropriate reading level on paper and screen, work with the children on developing and writing research questions. Support them in identifying key words and phrases in the questions and using these to focus their research.

Assessment

Listen to a radio news item and make effective notes for a particular purpose (feedback from other children, teacher observation).
Refer back to the learning outcomes on page 89.

Further work

Support children in making notes while listening to a radio broadcast by identifying suitable headings under which to group information. Draw attention to the use of key words and phrases rather than attempting to write out information in full.

DAY 1 ◼ Analysing newspaper articles

Key features	Stages	Additional opportunities
Enquiry: read and analyse a selection of newspaper articles	**Introduction** Remind the children of the work they have done so far on newspaper articles. **Speaking and listening** Ask the children to discuss, in pairs, what they have learned so far about paper-based news reports. Take feedback from the discussions, recapping particularly on their understanding of the five Ws (*Who? What? Where? When? Why?*). Explain that they are going to look in more detail at the way newspaper articles are organised and the language that is used. Show children an example of a newspaper article. Together, analyse the use of headlines to summarise the article, an introduction that usually includes some information about the five Ws, further detail about the event and the people involved in the body of the article. From this analysis, develop a writing frame that the children can use during the rest of the Unit. **Independent work** In pairs, children can repeat the analysis activity, using the articles from Phase 1, or others that you have identified. **Plenary** Discuss whether all of the articles they read followed the same structure.	**Extend:** some children can analyse online newspaper articles and establish the similarities and differences between these and paper-based articles

DAY 2 ◼ Analysing language features

Key features	Stages	Additional opportunities
Enquiry: read and analyse a selection of newspaper articles **Evaluation:** read, compare and evaluate news from a variety of sources	**Introduction** Remind the children of the work they did on analysing the structure of newspaper articles in the previous lesson. Explain that they are now going to look at the language features that are used. Return to the article you looked at together yesterday. Look at how the headline summarises the article and attracts the reader's attention. If appropriate, explore the use of word play and puns in headlines (photocopiable page 101 'Headlines' might be useful here). Note: sports reports and tabloid articles are more likely to contain these elements. Discuss the degree of formality of the article and, if appropriate, discuss how this varies depending on the type of paper – broadsheet or tabloid. Remind children that they already know about the five Ws used in articles. Focus on the use of action verbs and establish that news articles are written in the past tense. Finally, explore any evidence of bias in the article. For example, how the event is reported, who the quoted sources are, any obvious information that is left out. **Independent work** In pairs, children can repeat the language analysis, using the articles read in the previous lesson. **Plenary** Take feedback from the activity and discuss the children's findings. Are there any discrepancies that arise because of the source of the articles? Together look at any use of photographs and captions. What do the children think are the purpose of these?	

Guided reading
Using news articles from children's newspapers and/or news websites (copyright, NLA licence permitting), support the children in carrying out analyses of the structure and language features. Do these differ from the articles taken from adult newspapers and news websites?

Assessment
Identify what features and elements might be included in an effective written news report (teacher observation).
Refer back to the learning outcomes on page 89.

Further work
Support children in the analysis of typical language features by focusing on one element at a time. Give children a collection of newspaper articles with the headlines removed and given separately. Ask them to match the headlines with the associated articles. Discuss the techniques they used in order to do this.

DAY 1 ■ Planning a news article

Key features	Stages	Additional opportunities
	Introduction Remind the children that in Phase 2 they identified an event, about which they are going to write and record a radio broadcast. Discuss the audiences that they identified for their broadcasts.	
Evaluation: discuss success criteria	**Speaking and listening** In their groups, ask the children to consider how, having identified an audience for their broadcast, this will affect the tone, style and degree of formality of their broadcast. Encourage them to draw on the work they have done so far in the Unit during the discussion. As a class, develop two or three success criteria that the children will use to evaluate their broadcasts – both in terms of journalistic writing and presentation. Tell the children that they are going to plan and write their broadcast as an article before recording it. Identify an event that you are going to write about and the intended audience. Demonstrate how to plan it in note form using the writing frame developed in Day 1 of Phase 3 (see also photocopiable page 102 'News report writing frame').	
	Independent work Working in their groups, children can plan their news article.	**Extend:** as the children plan their article, ask them to note down any gaps in their information
	Plenary Take feedback from the planning activity. Are children clear about the structure?	

DAY 2 ■ Turning plans into notes

Key features	Stages	Additional opportunities
	Introduction Revisit the plan that you made in the previous lesson. Explain that, together, you are going to turn this into notes, thinking about the point of view of the article. Remind children of the work they did in Phase 2, thinking about bias in the articles they read. Discuss the point of view from which you are writing. Do you want to show one participant in the event in a good light and another in a poorer light? Decide on the approach that you are going to take and write the notes accordingly.	
Reasoning: construct reasoned arguments based on available information and evidence	**Speaking and listening** In their groups, children can decide on their point of view. Do they feel they have any gaps in their information?	
	Independent work Some children in the groups can focus on turning their plans into notes, still using photocopiable page 102 'News report writing frame' to structure the article. Others can carry out further research, in order to plug any gaps in the information they have. This could involve interviewing participants – real or imaginary, through face-to-face interviews, role play or hot-seating.	**Support:** help children by taking part in the role play and hot-seating yourself
Empathy: imagine oneself in another person's situation	**Plenary** Discuss progress with the groups. Do they feel that they have all of the information they need to move onto the next step of turning their notes into text? If not, build in more time for further research.	

DAY 3 ■ Writing an article

Key features	Stages	Additional opportunities
	Introduction Return to the notes that you made in the previous lesson. Explain that, together, you are going to turn this into a draft article. As a class, discuss how the audience will affect the style of the article and the point of view that you are going to take. Involve the children in writing the article. Revisit some of the news articles that have been read earlier in the Unit and explore the style and tone of the sources that have been used. Use these as models for quotes in your own writing. Remind children that if quotation marks are used, these are the exact words that the source used: *Mr Bloggs said, 'I am disgusted and appalled by what has happened'.* If it is reported speech, then it would be written slightly differently: *Mr Bloggs said that events had made him feel quite disgusted.*	
Communication: discuss and debate issues in respect of the articles being written	**Independent work** In their groups, children can turn their notes into a draft article. Ensure that they focus particularly on the use of reference to sources, either through direct or reported speech. **Plenary** Ask some of the groups to read their draft articles. Refer to the success criteria developed in Day 1 of this Phase to support the children in making any necessary changes. Ask the rest of the class to consider whether the point of view of the articles is clear. Could it be strengthened in any way? Work with the children on carrying out changes.	**Extend:** ask children to include references to participants in the event to add human interest to the articles

DAY 4 ■ Rehearsing broadcasts

Key features	Stages	Additional opportunities
Evaluation: comment critically on presentation techniques	**Introduction** Explain to the children that in this lesson they are going to rehearse their broadcasts and are going to concentrate on their presentation skills. Allow time for children to listen to some examples of radio news, asking them to focus on the broadcaster's use of pace, modulation and volume in their voice. Why do they think broadcasters use these techniques? Read out your article in a monotone and ask them to think about some guidance points that you could use to improve your performance. You may wish to draw up a list of similar points for the children to refer to as they rehearse.	
Communication: using discussion to reach a group agreement	**Speaking and listening** In their groups, children can take it in turns to read their articles, using the guidance points developed earlier. As a group, they can then decide on who should read the final broadcast. Encourage the groups to offer positive feedback and suggest ways that each reader can change and improve their presentations. Give the identified presenters the opportunity to record their broadcasts on hand-held recorders or computers with microphones. Are the presenters able to identify ways that they could improve their broadcasts? **Plenary** Ask the identified presenters in each group to feedback on particular guidance points that they found helpful. Were they surprised by anything when they heard themselves on the recordings?	**Extend:** give some children the opportunity to develop their audio broadcasts into visual presentations through videoing. Explore other aspects of presentation skills that are necessary (gestures, facial expression)

DAY 5 ■ Polishing and recording a broadcast

Key features	Stages	Additional opportunities
	Introduction Explain to the children that in this lesson they are going to have a last opportunity to polish their presentations before making the final recording.	
	Independent work In groups, children can read through their articles, discussing and making final editorial changes. Encourage them to consider clarity of information and words that they feel could be changed to add more impact to the article. Encourage them to consider what changes they will need to make to turn the written articles into effective spoken texts.	
Communication: communicate orally through recorded broadcasts	**Speaking and listening** The presenters can rehearse their broadcasts in front of two or three of the group. Encourage the listeners to comment on the presenter's pace, audibility and expression. Can they suggest specific changes that can be made to enhance the presentation and to ensure that the listeners will be engaged? If necessary, give the children the opportunity to listen to the radio broadcasts again. Carry out the recordings of the broadcasts.	**Support:** give some groups time limits for their presentations. Ask them to edit their articles so that the final broadcasts fit the time frame
Evaluate: judge the effectiveness of broadcasts against established success criteria	**Plenary** Play the broadcasts to the class and ask them to use the success criteria developed in Day 1 of this Phase to evaluate them. Where possible, play the broadcasts to the intended audience and encourage the children to ask for, and to discuss, the audience's responses. Explore with the children what they think they have learned during this Unit.	

Guided reading
Support the children in structuring their written articles and in capturing the reader's and listener's attention in the opening few lines.

Assessment
Write and present an effective news report, making appropriate choices regarding language, style, structure and presentation relating to purpose and audience (marking and feedback against agreed success criteria).
Ask children to complete the CD-ROM assessment activity 'Journalistic writing evaluation'.
Refer back to the learning outcomes on page 89.

Further work
Give children the opportunity to write for, and present to, a variety of audiences, using various modes of presentation (written, audio and visual).

Name _____   Date _____

Identifying information in news articles

■ Use these headings to make notes about a newspaper article or news broadcast. Try to be as detailed as possible.

Where did the event happen?

Why did the event happen?

Article or news broadcast

When was the article written/broadcast?

What is the story about? What happened?

■ Answer the following on the back of the sheet.

1. Do you think the article/broadcast gave you enough information?

2. What did you like/dislike about the article/broadcast?

3. How would you improve the article/broadcast?

PHOTOCOPIABLE ■SCHOLASTIC
www.scholastic.co.uk

Headlines

■ Use these headlines for ideas to create your own news article. You could change the wording of the headline when you have written your article.

Holiday-makers warned of sun-bathing dangers

Pop star quits music for motherhood

Valuable antiques stolen from historic castle

Savage storm causes chaos

Guide dog saves owner from fire

New planet discovered in solar system

Name _____   Date _____

News report writing frame

■ Use this frame to help you plan your news article.

Headline (To summarise the article)

Length (How long will your article be? Approx number of words/how many paragraphs/pages)

Type of newspaper/intended audience (Will it be a tabloid or a broadsheet article? Who will be the main readers?)

Introduction (Include who, what, where, when, why)

Body (More detail about the event/detail about the people involved)

Subheading (Will your article have subheadings? How many?)

Quotes (Will you use quotes? If so how many and who will you be quoting?)

Image (Will your article have images/photos? If so what will the images be of and why will you be using them? Will they be colour or black and white?)

Caption (Will the images have captions? What will these say?)

■ 100 LITERACY FRAMEWORK LESSONS YEAR 6

PHOTOCOPIABLE ■SCHOLASTIC
www.scholastic.co.uk

NON-FICTION
UNIT 3 Argument

Speak and listen for a range on purposes on paper and on screen

Strand 1 Speaking
■ Use a range of oral techniques to present persuasive arguments and engaging narratives.
■ Participate in whole-class debate using the conventions and language of debate, including standard English.
Strand 2 Listening and responding
■ Analyse and evaluate how speakers present points effectively through use of language and gesture.
■ Listen for language variation in formal and informal contexts.
■ Identify the ways spoken language varies according to differences in the context and purpose of use.

Read for a range of purposes on paper and on screen

Strand 6 Word structure and spelling
■ Use a range of appropriate strategies to edit, proofread and correct spelling in their own work, on paper and on screen.
Strand 7 Understanding and interpreting texts
■ Recognise rhetorical devices used to argue, persuade, mislead and sway the reader.
Strand 8 Engaging with and responding to texts
■ Compare how writers from different times and places present experiences and use language.

Write for a range of purposes on paper and on screen

Strand 9 Creating and shaping texts
■ In non-narrrative, establish, balance and maintain viewpoints.
Strand 10 Text structure and organisation
■ Use varied structures to shape and organise text coherently.
■ Use paragraphs to achieve pace and emphasis.
Strand 11 Sentence structure and punctuation
■ Use punctuation to clarify meaning in complex sentences.
Strand 12 Presentation
■ Use different styles of handwriting for different purposes with a range of media, developing a consistent and personal legible style.

Progression in discussion texts

In this year children are moving towards:
■ Identifying the language , grammar, organisational and stylistic features of balanced written discussions which:
  – summarise different sides of an argument
  – signal personal opinion clearly
  – draw reasoned conclusions based on available evidence.
■ Recognising and understanding the distinction between the persuasive presentation of a particular view and the discursive presentation of a balanced argument.
■ Exploring orally and writing a balanced report of an issue.
■ Using reading to investigate conditionals and their persuasive uses.

UNIT 3 ◀ Argument *continued*

■ Helping to build the ability to choose the appropriate style and form to suit a specific purpose and audience, drawing on knowledge of different non-fiction text types and adapting these where appropriate.

Key aspects of learning covered in this Unit

Enquiry
Children will identify the particular information, ideas and opinions offered in different texts, asking questions such as: *What does this particular writer think, and why? Do others think the same?*

Information processing
Children will source, collate and analyse information, ideas and opinions offered in different texts and media presentations.

Evaluation
Children will examine a variety of arguments and discussions, weighing evidence and evaluating both effectiveness and appropriateness for context. The same elements will then be explored in terms of their own speaking and writing.

Reasoning
Children will follow and evaluate the arguments of others, and then construct and evaluate their own reasoning both orally and in writing.

Communication
They will develop their ability to discuss and debate issues from both a biased and a balanced standpoint. They will often work collaboratively in pairs and groups. They will communicate ideas and opinions orally, in writing and through using other modes and media.

Prior learning

Before starting this Unit check that the children can:
■ Identify and discuss elements of persuasion when they encounter them
■ Recognise the difference between the expression of a particular viewpoint and the presentation of a balanced discussion.
■ Understand how texts are and can be adapted to suit different purposes and audiences.
■ Use clear language to present a spoken argument or point of view.
If they need further support please refer to a prior Unit or a similar Unit in Year 5.

Resources

Phase 1:
Chips Get the Chop! by Gerry Bailey ✾; Interview with someone about healthy eating; *Healthier food for school children* by Gerry Bailey ✾; Interactive activity 'Parent power' ✾

Phase 2:
Photocopiable page 117 'Evaluating presentations'; Photocopiable page 118 'Planning an argument'

Phase 3:
Mobile phone: friend or foe? by Gill Matthews ✾; Persuasion skeleton; Photocopiable page 118 'Planning an argument'; Assessment activity 'Persuasive letter' ✾

Cross-curricular opportunities

Persuasive and discursive texts about issues raised in other curricular areas.

UNIT 3 ■ Teaching sequence

Phase	Children's objectives	Summary of activities	Learning outcomes
1	I can identify and analyse a point of view. I can identify formal and informal language. I can identify effective persuasive points.	Sorting texts according to point of view. Comparing texts. Text highlighting. Role play.	Children can identify bias and appropriate use of formal language.
2	I can evaluate discussion and presentations.	Group discussion. Whole class formal discussion. Summarising discussions.	Children can use clear language and appropriate presentational features both to present a case and provide a balanced discussion.
3	I can analyse persuasive and discussion texts. I can identify formal language.	Text analysis.	Children can recognise the structure and language features of a persuasive argument and a balanced discussion. Children can understand and apply impersonal and formal language when appropriate.
4	I can develop success criteria. I can plan and write persuasive and discussion texts.	Group discussion. Paired writing.	Children can write an effective argument for a particular case and a balanced discussion of an issue, selecting language, form, format and content to suit a particular audience and purpose.

Provide copies of the objectives for the children.

DAY 1 ▪ Exploring point of view

Key features	Stages	Additional opportunities
	### Introduction Explain to the children that in this Unit they will be exploring texts that present balanced and biased points of view, referred to as discussion/argument and persuasive texts. Discuss the children's existing knowledge of these text types. Remind them of the recent debate over the junk food ban in schools and discuss any impact they have noticed in school and at home. With the children, read through the newspaper article *Chips Get the Chop!* from the CD-ROM. Do they think it is for, against or balanced about the junk food ban? Encourage them to refer to the text for evidence to support their responses.	
	### Speaking and listening In groups, ask the children to discuss their views on the junk food ban in schools. Ask each group to appoint a spokesperson to feed back the group's views. Take feedback and discuss the issue as a class.	**Support:** appoint scribes for each group, asking them to note down the main points in the discussion
Enquiry: identify information, ideas and opinions that support a particular point of view	### Independent work Give children access to *Chips Get the Chop!* and *Healthier food for school children* from the CD-ROM. Others can explore the internet to find further examples of articles, both in written and visual forms (copyright permitting). Ask them to sort them into three groups: for, against and balanced.	
	### Plenary Discuss the sorting activity. What evidence in the texts did the children use to group the texts?	

DAY 2 ▪ Exploring formal and informal language

Key features	Stages	Additional opportunities
	### Introduction Remind children of the sorting activity they did in the previous lesson. Was any particular group of texts larger than the others? Do they think that this reflects the general view of the junk food ban? Are they aware of the celebrity chef, Jamie Oliver, who played a big part in bringing the issue of healthy eating to the public's notice? What do they know about him?	
Enquiry: identify information and evidence	### Independent work In pairs or small groups, ask the children to find and read an interview with Jamie Oliver or another interview on the same subject. They should focus on finding evidence of the levels of formality and the use of personal and impersonal language.	**Extend:** some children could look at some of Jamie Oliver's recipes to analyse the informal
Evaluation: examining degrees of formality	### Plenary Focus on the interview that the children have investigated during the independent work. Explore the use of informal language in the interview compared with the more formal language in the newspaper article *Healthier food for school children* from the CD-ROM.	nature of his writing compared to other celebrity chefs

DAY 3 ◢ Analysing point of view

Key features	Stages	Additional opportunities
	Introduction Explain to the children that they are going to read a newspaper article that reports the actions some parents took following the introduction of healthy eating in one school. Complete the interactive activity 'Parent power' from the CD-ROM with the children. Ask them to think about the parents' actions as you read. Do they think the mothers were right to do what they did?	
Evaluation: examine arguments and discussions, weighing evidence presented in the text	**Independent work** Give the children copies of the completed activity. In pairs, they can analyse the article, highlighting the mothers' points of view and reasons for their actions in one colour and any opposing points of view in another colour. **Plenary** Look at the highlighting marks the children have made on their copies of the article. Do the children feel that the article is biased in favour of the mothers, or do they feel that the information is presented in a balanced way? As a class, discuss whether the children feel that the actions of the mothers were justified. Do they think that the reasons given for the mothers' behaviour were convincing? What do they think is the main argument put forward by the two women? Discuss the views presented by the school involved. Who is the school's spokesperson? Do the children think that the newspaper should have interviewed anyone else in order to present an alternative point of view?	**Extend:** ask some pairs to focus on the quotes from those involved in the event and to identify any similarities and differences

DAY 4 ◢ Exploring persuasion through role play

Key features	Stages	Additional opportunities
	Introduction Remind the children of the article they read in the previous lesson. Ask them to consider what could lie behind the mothers' actions. Re-read the article together. Do the children feel that these arguments are valid? Consider how they could be strengthened, for example by quotes from other parents and the children.	
Reasoning: discuss and debate issues persuasively	**Speaking and listening** Ask the children to work in small groups for a role-play activity. They should explore conversations that might have gone on between the mothers, local parents and their children, in which the parents and children were trying to persuade the mothers to set up the food delivery service. Each group should nominate an observer who notes down the main persuasive points of the conversation. In their groups, led by the observers, the children can discuss the more effective points that were raised and their use of persuasive words and phrases. **Plenary** Take feedback from the role-play activity and discussion. Establish which persuasive methods were effective. Broaden the discussion to include situations when the children have tried to persuade their parents of something. Explain that a well constructed persuasive argument can often be more effective than nagging.	

Guided reading
Give children examples of discursive texts that offer balanced arguments about an issue. Support them in identifying both sides of the argument. Compare these with texts that are clearly biased in favour of one side of an issue.

Assessment
Appraise a discussion text and evaluate whether it is presenting a biased or balanced point of view (teacher observation, self-assessment).
Refer back to the learning outcomes on page 105.

Further work
Encourage children to be critical readers, identifying evidence of bias as they read. Support them in looking for evidence in texts and also identifying any key information that is missing.

DAY 1 ■ Evaluating presentations

Key features	Stages	Additional opportunities
	Introduction Before this lesson, brief three children and allow them time to prepare their discussion. They should identify an issue that they want to discuss then prepare presentations that explore two differing viewpoints. As the two viewpoints are presented, the third child in the group can take notes. After the presentation, the note-taker can summarise the key points in a balanced, impartial manner.	
Reasoning: follow and evaluate the arguments of others	**Speaking and listening** Ask children to work in small groups. Each group should identify a chairperson who will run the discussion, a timekeeper and a note-taker who will work with a spokesperson. Explain that they have 15 minutes to discuss the presentation that they have just seen. They should consider the points that each speaker raised, the effectiveness of those points and of the summary. Give the note-taker and spokesperson time to prepare feedback on the group discussion.	**Support:** work with children, listing the points presented in two columns headed for and against, in order to differentiate between the points of view
Evaluate: analyse content of presentations	**Plenary** Take feedback from the group discussions. As a class, develop a list of criteria for making successful presentations, particularly focusing on presenting effective points of view. Encourage the children to consider the order of the points raised, the importance of supporting opinions with reasons and evidence, the need for a balanced summary of the points presented. Broaden the discussion to include general presentation skills – for example, speaking clearly and audibly, using expression, incorporating facial and hand gestures.	

DAY 2 ■ Evaluating discussion

Key features	Stages	Additional opportunities
	Introduction Discuss and identify potential issues for group discussions. These could be issues that are relevant to the children and the school, or issues related to other curricular areas such as child labour during Victorian times, or pedestrianisation of the town centre. Remind children of the discussion they observed in the previous lesson and the three roles that the children involved adopted. Revisit the criteria established during the previous plenary session.	
Evaluation: examine a variety of arguments and discussions **Reasoning:** follow and evaluate the arguments of others	**Speaking and listening** Ask the children to work in groups of four. They should choose an issue to discuss. Two children can prepare and present two opposing sides of the issue, one child can take notes and summarise the discussion, the fourth should act as observer – analysing the impartiality of the summary and considering the criteria for presenting effective points of view in the context of the group work. **Plenary** Ask the observer from each group to report back on their group's discussion. Focus particularly on the evaluation of the fairness and effectiveness of the summing up. As a class, discuss what the children think are the important attributes of each of the roles in the group. Do any of the participants think that they would have been more effective in a different role? Why? Did they encounter any problems in thinking of arguments to support a particular point of view? Establish that it is easier to argue a point of view if you feel strongly about it.	**Support:** work with the group, identifying the key points of the issue they are discussing and supporting them in structuring their discussion effectively

DAY 3 ◀ Whole-class formal discussion

Key features	Stages	Additional opportunities
	## Introduction	
	Remind the children of the issue they explored in Phase 1 – the ban on junk food in schools. Remind them of the situation in school regarding junk food, and what the children are allowed to bring in lunch boxes or for snacks. Explain to the children that they are going to have a formal discussion on the issue, for example the house believes that children should have free choice to eat what they wish for their snacks. Appoint teams to speak for and against the statement, 'expert witnesses' to provide evidence for the teams, a chairperson who will summarise the discussion and a panel who will make the final decision based on the evidence they hear. Revisit the criteria established in Day 1 of this Phase and remind the children to bear these in mind during the discussion. It would be helpful to record (either audio or video) the forthcoming whole-class discussion. (Ensure you get parents' or carers' permission before taking photographs or filming.)	
Reasoning: follow and evaluate the arguments of others. Construct and evaluate their own reasoning	## Speaking and listening Give the teams time to gather their evidence and to prepare their statements. Tell them that they have a limited time to present their arguments, maybe five minutes per team. Carry out the formal discussion; allow the chairperson to summarise and the panel to come to a decision, based on what they have heard.	**Support:** work with the panel, supporting them in making a decision based on the evidence they have heard rather than any emotion they might feel
	## Plenary Ask the children to reflect individually on the discussion and whether they feel the final decision was just.	

DAY 4 ◀ Evaluating the effectiveness of presentations

Key features	Stages	Additional opportunities
Evaluation: weigh evidence and evaluate discussions in terms of effectiveness and appropriateness	## Introduction Remind the children of the criteria against which they can evaluate presentations. Play the recording of the class discussion held the previous day. Ask the children to consider: ■ the effectiveness of the individual presentations – Were they persuasive? Were they based on evidence or hearsay? ■ the summary by the chairperson – Did it take both sides of the discussion into consideration? Was it impartial? ■ the decision by the panel – Was it a fair conclusion?	
	## Speaking and listening In small groups, the children can consider and discuss the points raised above. Each group should prepare a brief summary of their discussion. Encourage them to structure their summary by making statements and then supporting the statements with evidence taken from the whole class discussion.	**Support:** some groups could use photocopiable page 117 'Evaluating presentations' to structure their summaries
Communication: work collaboratively	## Plenary Take feedback from each of the groups, allowing the rest of the class to challenge any statements that they feel are unfair, biased or lack supporting evidence. In the light of the groups' feedback, do the children feel that the criteria for evaluating presentations should be changed in any way?	

Guided writing

Work with children, and groups, in structuring point of view and presentations and using supporting arguments. Some children could use photocopiable page 118 'Planning an argument' to plan their arguments.

Assessment

Speak in a clear, interesting and persuasive way, when presenting a particular point of view (feedback from other children, teacher observation).

Refer back to the learning outcomes on page 105.

Further work

Give individual children the choice of three subjects and ask them to speak for a minute on their chosen subject without hesitation, repetition or deviation. You may wish to reduce the time to 30 seconds for some children.

DAY 1 ◼ Analysing persuasive texts

Key features	Stages	Additional opportunities

Introduction

Remind the children that so far in this Unit, they have been thinking about presenting balanced arguments, or giving two or more points of view about an issue during discussions. Ask the children what they know about spoken and written texts that only put forward one point of view. What is the purpose of this kind of text (to persuade) and what text type is it (persuasive)? Explain that, generally, persuasive texts try to persuade the reader to do, say, think or buy something – sometimes against their better judgement. Activate children's prior knowledge of the typical structural and linguistic features of persuasive texts. List these on the board.

Evaluation: examine and evaluate a variety of persuasive texts

Independent work

Give the children some examples of persuasive texts. In groups, ask them to analyse the structure of the texts and to list some of the language features that they notice. They should refer to the class list produced earlier in the lesson to support this activity.

Plenary

Take feedback from the group activity. Add any further features that the children have identified to the earlier class list. Lead the children towards the understanding that a discursive text is really two or more persuasive arguments or points of view.

Extend: give children examples of persuasive and discursive texts; ask them to list the similarities and differences between the two text types

DAY 2 ◼ Analysing discussion texts

Key features	Stages	Additional opportunities

Introduction

Remind the children of the amount of work they have done so far in this Unit on analysing oral discussions. Ask them to tell you what they know about oral, or spoken, discussions. When and why are they used? Who might use them? List the children's responses. Explore the kind of language used in oral discussions. If necessary, revisit the recording of the class discussion from Day 3 of Phase 2 to support this activity. Add typical language features to the list.

Evaluation: examine and evaluate a variety of discussion texts

Independent work

Give children, in small groups, examples of discussion texts. Ask them to analyse the structure of the texts and to list some of the language features that they notice. They should refer to the class list produced earlier in the lesson to support this activity.

Plenary

Take feedback from the group activity. Add any further features that the children have identified to the earlier class list. Discuss the key differences between these discussion texts and the persuasive texts analysed in the previous lesson. Ensure that the children have a clear understanding of the similarities and differences between the two text types, particularly the differing purposes of the two texts. As a class, produce definitions for the two text types. Discuss when and why the children might read and write discussion and persuasive texts.

Support: work with the children on identifying the structure and language features of the texts. You may wish to ask them to carry out text marking or highlighting activities

DAY 3 ◼ Identifying formal language

Key features	Stages	Additional opportunities
	Introduction Explain to the children that they are going to compare another discussion text with some they have looked at previously. Show them the discussion text *Mobile phone: friend or foe?* from the CD-ROM.	
Evaluation: examine and evaluate a variety of discussion texts	**Speaking and listening** Ask the children to read through the discussion text and to discuss, in pairs, any structural and linguistic similarities to other texts they have read. Take feedback, listing the children's responses. Draw the children's attention to the impersonal nature of the language and how this makes it a more formal text.	**Support:** work with the children on highlighting formal and informal language in two examples of discussion texts
	Independent work In pairs, ask the children to investigate the formal nature of the language, listing examples they find.	
	Plenary Take feedback and compare the language with other more informal examples.	

Guided reading

Work with the children on analysing persuasive and discursive texts, supporting them in identifying the differing purposes, structures and language features. Ensure that they are secure in their understanding of each text type.

Assessment

Identify what features and elements might be included in a persuasive argument and in a balanced discussion (teacher observation).
Refer back to the learning outcomes on page 105.

Further work

Give children opportunities to prepare an oral persuasive presentation on an issue that they feel strongly about. Ask other children to listen carefully to the points presented and to construct an opposing argument.

DAY 1 ■ Developing success criteria

Key features	Stages	Additional opportunities
	Introduction Remind the children that the issue they have been exploring in this Unit is the introduction of the ban on junk food in schools. They have been doing this by looking at persuasive texts that present one point of view and discussion texts that offer one or more points of view. They have also looked at the use of formal and informal language.	
Communication: work collaboratively in small groups	**Independent work** Working in small groups, ask the children to think about what they know about the two text types. They can then develop a list of success criteria that they could use to judge the effectiveness of their own writing in these two areas.	**Support:** ask children to focus on one text type **Extend:** encourage children to consider how the audience for a text might affect the success criteria
	Plenary Take feedback from the group discussions and produce a list of success criteria for each text type that will be used to evaluate the success of the children's writing later in the Unit. Through discussion based on the texts read during this Unit, develop a list of points for and against the ban on junk foods. Encourage the children to add their own views to the list. Display the list for reference during the rest of the Unit.	

DAY 2 ■ Planning and writing persuasive texts

Key features	Stages	Additional opportunities
	Introduction Remind the children of the features of a persuasive text and the success criteria developed in the previous lesson. Display the Persuasion skeleton from the CD-ROM and explore with the children how it can support the planning of a text. Identify the issue that you are going to write about. Ask the children to briefly discuss the issue in pairs. Use the Persuasion skeleton to plan the text. Identify an audience for the text. Demonstrate how to turn the plan into continuous text. Involve the children in drawing on their knowledge of the typical language features of persuasive texts, based on those they have read in this Unit and others.	
	Speaking and listening Ask the children, working in pairs, to choose an issue that they wish to write about persuasively. Give them time to discuss and note down what they know about the issue and to identify any gaps in their knowledge.	
Reasoning: construct and evaluate own reasoning	**Independent work** Allow children time to carry out any further research into their chosen issue. They can then use photocopiable page 118 'Planning an argument' to plan their text, turning it eventually into continuous persuasive text for a specific audience.	**Support:** allow children time to plan their texts orally before writing them
	Plenary Ask some pairs to read their texts. Encourage the rest of the class to use the success criteria to evaluate the texts.	

DAY 3 ■ Planning and writing discussion texts

Key features	Stages	Additional opportunities
	Introduction Explain that in this lesson you are going to plan and write a discussion text. Return to, and read through, the persuasive text written in the previous lesson.	
	Speaking and listening In pairs, ask children to develop a list of points that oppose the views in the persuasive text. Demonstrate how to plan a text that incorporates two or more points of view of the issue. Remind the children of the language features of a discussion text. Incorporate these as you turn the notes into continuous text for an identified audience.	
Reasoning: construct and evaluate own reasoning	**Independent work** Ask the children to return to their persuasive texts written in the previous lesson. In their pairs, they can develop a list of opposing or alternative points of view. They can repeat the planning and writing activity demonstrated in this lesson, turning their plans into continuous discussion texts for a particular audience.	**Support:** allow children time to plan their texts orally before writing them
	Plenary Ask some children to read their discussion texts. Use the success criteria developed in Day 1 of this Phase to evaluate the texts.	

DAY 4 ■ Refining and redrafting discussion texts

Key features	Stages	Additional opportunities
	Introduction Remind the children of the work they have done in this Unit on formal and informal language and the impact of using formal language on a text and on the reader. Return to the discussion text that you wrote in the previous lesson. Read through it and, with the children, identify opportunities for using more formal language. Refine the text and re-read it, discussing the impact of the changes made.	
Reasoning: construct and evaluate own reasoning	**Speaking and listening** Ask pairs of children to work together in groups of four. Each pair of children should present their discussion text, written in the previous lesson, to their partners. Encourage the children to consider further arguments that could be added to the text to strengthen the points being made.	
	Independent work Ask the children to identify an audience for their texts. In pairs, they can redraft their discussion texts in the light of the points raised by their partners.	**Extend:** support children in structuring their discussion texts in a more sophisticated way – alternating arguments and counter-arguments, rather than grouping them together
	Plenary As a class, discuss the changes the children have made to their discussion texts and the impact these have had. Use the success criteria to evaluate the children's writing. Together, talk about what the children understand and know about persuasive and discursive writing, the purpose of each text type, when they might write them and why.	

Guided reading

Support the children in structuring their persuasive and discursive texts and using appropriate language. Focus particularly on the use of emotive language in persuasion and objectivity in discussion.

Assessment

Write an effective persuasive argument and balanced discussion, making appropriate language, style and structural choices to meet a particular purpose and audience (marking and feedback against agreed success criteria).

Ask the children to complete the CD-ROM assessment activity 'Persuasive letter'.

Refer back to the learning outcomes on page 105.

Further work

Give the children opportunities to write persuasive and discursive texts for different audiences. Focus on how the audience can affect the use of formal and informal language.

Evaluating presentations

■ Complete the presentation evaluation below. You may wish to use the words in the box below to help you.

We feel that _____'s presentation was _____.

This is because _____

The evidence they used was _____

_____

_____

We feel that the chairperson's summary was _____

This is because _____

_____

_____

We feel that the panel's decision was _____

This is because _____

_____

_____

Overall, we feel that the discussion was _____

This is because _____

_____

_____

Useful words and phrases

detailed, descriptive, interesting, long, short, boring, clear, quick, slow, understand, easy, hard, clear, complicated, specific, fair, unfair, right, wrong, justified, wonderful, structure, good, bad, obvious, variety, biased, points of view

Name _____   Date _____

Planning an argument

■ **What is the issue/topic of your argument?**

■ **Our/my argument**

In this box write the reasons for your argument. Include your feelings, facts, opinions, evidence and conclusion.

_____

_____

_____

_____

_____

_____

_____

_____

_____

_____

_____

_____

_____

■ **The opposition**

In this box think of the reasons why others may oppose your arguments and what their opinions might be.

_____

_____

_____

_____

_____

_____

_____

_____

_____

_____

_____

_____

NON-FICTION
UNIT 4 Formal/impersonal writing

Speak and listen for a range on purposes on paper and on screen

Strand 1 Speaking
- Use the techniques of dialogic talk to explore ideas, topics or issues.

Strand 2 Listening and responding
- Identify the ways spoken language varies according to differences in the context and purpose of its use.

Strand 3 Group discussion and interaction
- Understand and use a variety of ways to criticise constructively and respond to criticism.

Read for a range of purposes on paper and on screen

Strand 6 Word structure and spelling
- Use a range of appropriate strategies to edit, proofread and correct spelling in their own work, on paper and on screen.

Strand 7 Understanding and interpreting texts
- Understand how writers use different structures to create coherence and impact.

Strand 8 Engaging with and responding to texts
- Compare how writers from different times and places present experiences and use language.

Write for a range of purposes on paper and on screen

Strand 9 Creating and shaping texts
- Set own challenges to extend achievement and experience in writing.
- Select words and language drawing on their knowledge of literary features and formal and informal writing.
- Integrate words, images and sounds imaginatively for different purposes.

Strand 10 Text structure and organisation
- Use varied structures to shape and organise texts coherently.

Strand 11 Sentence structure and punctuation
- Express subtle distinctions of meaning, including hypothesis, speculation and supposition, by constructing sentences in varied ways.
- Use punctuation to clarify meaning in complex sentences.

Strand 12 Presentation
- Select from a wide range of ICT programs to present text effectively and communicate information and ideas.

Progression in information texts

In this year children are moving towards:
- Appraising a text quickly, deciding on its value, quality or usefulness; evaluating the language, style and effectiveness of examples of non-fiction writing.
- Writing information texts, selecting the appropriate style and form to suit a specific purpose and audience, drawing on knowledge of different non-fiction text types.
- Revising own non-fiction writing to reduce superfluous words and phrases.

UNIT 4 ◀ Formal/impersonal writing *continued*

Key aspects of learning covered in this Unit

Enquiry
Children will seek the answers to their own and others' questions in their activity throughout this Unit.

Information processing
Children will identify relevant information from a range of sources and use this as a basis for writing or presentation. They will explore and tease out the elements involved in combined, conflated and multimodal text types.

Evaluation
Children will compare and evaluate the effectiveness of a wide range of non-fiction texts and presentations. They will share their own writing and presentation outcomes, discuss success criteria, give feedback to others and judge the effectiveness of their own work.

Communication
Children will develop their ability to discuss effective communication in respect of both the form and the content of the non-fiction texts they are reading and creating. They will often work collaboratively in pairs and groups. They will communicate outcomes orally and in writing.

Prior learning

Before starting this Unit check that the children can:
■ Recall the language and organisational features of the main non-fiction text types (recount, report, instructions, explanation, persuasion, discussion) and employ these in their writing, when appropriate.
■ Understand that non-fiction can sometimes employ a hybrid of text types and forms, depending on its audience and purpose.
■ Understand something of how to integrate words, images and sounds together into a multimodal text (and how to achieve this in practice in an ICT context).
If they need further support please refer to a prior Unit or a similar Unit in Year 5.

Resources

Phase 1:
Guides to a number of locations – written, audio, visual, virtual; Photocopiable page 132 'Analysing guides'
Phase 2:
Photocopiable page 133 'Planning interviews'
Phase 3:
No additional resources required
Phase 4:
Photocopiable page 134 'Planning a guide flatplan'; Assessment activity 'Guides – self evaluation' ✆

Cross-curricular opportunities

Geography
History
Links to other subject areas by asking children to produce guides based on places that are, or have been, studied in geography and places and times that have been explored through history.

UNIT 4 ■ Teaching sequence

Phase	Children's objectives	Summary of activities	Learning outcomes
1	I can identify audience and purpose. I can identify how information is presented.	Group discussion and text analysis.	Children can understand how non-fiction information can be presented in a number of formats. Children can evaluate the effectiveness of the language, organisation and presentational features of specific non-fiction texts.
2	I can identify a location, content and an audience for a guide.	Group discussion. Interviewing and role play.	Children can use a wide range of discussion and role-taking techniques to explore non-fiction subject matter.
3	I can research information. I can plot a route. I can identify presentational features.	Developing research questions. Making visual representations. Group discussion and allocation of responsibilities.	Children can research and assemble information from a variety of sources. Children can plan a presentation of non-fiction information.
4	I can develop success criteria. I can plan, draft, revise, edit and complete guides. I can evaluate guides.	Planning, revising, presenting and evaluating as a group. Drafting and editing individually and as a group. Working collaboratively.	Children can evaluate work against agreed success criteria.

Provide copies of the objectives for the children.

DAY 1 ■ Exploring purpose and audience

Key features	Stages	Additional opportunities
	Introduction In preparation for this Unit you will need to gather together guides to a number of locations. These need to represent the various guide formats that are available such as written guide books, audio guides, video guides and virtual guides. If possible, integrate a visit to a particular location into this first Phase of the Unit. Explain to the children that during this Unit they will be exploring and developing guides to a particular place. Explore the children's existing knowledge of guides: have they been on a guided tour, used guide books, explored virtual tours?	
Communication: working collaboratively in groups and in role	**Speaking and listening** Ask the children to work in groups of about six. You may wish to suggest friendship or mixed ability groups. Explain that they will be working in these groups for the rest of the Unit. Each group should nominate a chairperson, note-taker, spokesperson and timekeeper. Establish the responsibility of each of these roles. Give the groups a time limit in which they can discuss why they think guides are produced and who they are for (purpose and audience).	**Extend:** ask two or three children to circulate and observe the group members in action
	Plenary Ask the spokesperson for each group to give feedback on their discussions. Develop a class list of the audience and purpose of guides, such as visitors who want to know how to find their way around, to tell visitors about the most interesting parts of the place. As a class, discuss the roles and responsibilities of group members. Explore the qualities needed for each role and how effectively the roles were carried out.	**Extend:** ask the observers for feedback on their observations

DAY 2 ■ Analysing written guides

Key features	Stages	Additional opportunities
	Introduction Introduce the locations that you have identified as the focus for this Unit and the various formats of guides that you have collected together. Are any of the children familiar with the locations? If appropriate, discuss their experiences of visiting them. Were they given a guided tour or did they use a guide? If so, what was the format of the guide? How effective do they feel the guides were?	
Information processing: identify how information is presented in written guides	**Independent work** Remind the children of the groups they worked in during the previous lesson. Do they wish to retain the roles or give other children the opportunity to take them on? Give each group of children an example of a text-based guide. Ask them to read these carefully and to identify and list the information that is given visually (maps, photographs, timetables, colour coding, diagrams). What extra or similar information is given in the text? They can also consider the specific audience and purpose of the guides. Let the children use photocopiable page 132 'Analysing guides' when undertaking this task.	**Support:** work with the children in 'reading' the visual elements in the guide
	Plenary Take feedback from each group. Discuss how much information was presented visually. Are there any significant similarities and differences between the various guides? Explore the audience for each guide (usually the general public). Are any of the guides aimed at a specific audience, such as people with a particular interest or hobby, older adults, children? Discuss the purpose of the guides – is there any evidence of persuasion in them?	

DAY 3 ■ Analysing visual and audio guides

Key features	Stages	Additional opportunities
	Introduction Remind the children of their analysis of written guides in the previous lesson. Return to the purpose of the guides – they were giving information about the location, as in a non-chronological report, and at times persuading people to visit. Did the children find any evidence of other text types, such as instructions?	
Information processing: identify how information is presented in written guides	**Independent work** Give each group of children an example of a video, audio or virtual guide. Ask them to explore these and to identify any similarities and differences between these and the written guides explored in the previous lesson. Each group should consider how the information is presented, for example use of visuals, audio, text, the audience for, and purpose of, each guide. Photocopiable page 132 'Analysing guides' will help them with this task.	**Extend:** focus children's attention on evidence of different text types in the guides by thinking about the effect it has on them as a viewer, listener and/or reader
	Plenary Take feedback from each group. Through discussion, establish which format the children prefer and the reasons for their preferences. Which format did they find most informative? Have the children been able to identify the audience and purpose? Refer them back to the discussion about the purpose of guides in the previous lesson. Did they identify any evidence of different text types? Discuss this evidence and establish that a text type can occur in written, visual and audio texts. Broaden the discussion to include who might prefer to use a video or audio guide and when they might be used. For example, before a visit to establish particular places someone might want to see, or during a visit to help them find their way round.	

Guided writing

Support children in analysing the relationship between text and visuals and the information given in visuals by producing a graphic outline. A graphic outline is a drawn representation of a page or double page spread in which boxes are used to indicate the position of text, including captions, and visuals. Children can then make notes summarising the information that is given in each box. Discuss with the children which elements they read first (visuals or text) and how these relate to each other.

Assessment

Recognise the key elements of non-fiction text types, when they are presented as mixed text types and multimodal formats (teacher observation and feedback).
Refer back to the learning outcomes on page 121.

Further work

Involve children in text-marking activities in which they identify and highlight in different colours the various text types within a written text. Establish that thinking about the purpose of a section of text can help in identifying the text type.

DAY 1 ■ Identifying a focus for a guide

Key features	Stages	Additional opportunities
	### Introduction With the children, discuss the various formats of guides, the audiences that they have identified and the varied purposes of the guides that they have explored so far. If the children have had the opportunity to be taken on a guided tour of a particular location, discuss the experience, focusing specifically on the information the guide gave them and how it was delivered and received. Explore the impact and experience of a real-life guided tour and a computer-based virtual tour. Which do the children prefer, and why?	
Communication: work collaboratively and come to a group decision	### Speaking and listening In their groups, ask the children to consider and identify a location on which they are going to base their guide. This could be a location that is easily accessible, such as the school; linked to another curricular area, such as a town in Victorian or Second World War times; fictional or imaginary, such as a newly discovered planet or land. You may wish to guide particular groups towards choosing an appropriate location. Once they have identified a location, the groups can establish the specific audience for their guide, the purpose of the guide and the format it will take – video, audio, virtual, visual, written (or a mix of these). Encourage the groups to draw on their experience of the various guides and their features during the previous three lessons.	**Support:** ensure the children are realistic in their expectations of what they are able to produce, given the time and resources available
	### Plenary Talk about and establish an appropriate audience, purpose and format for each group's guide.	

DAY 2 ■ Exploring intended content of a guide

Key features	Stages	Additional opportunities
	### Introduction Discuss with the children how they intend to collect information about their chosen location. If necessary, revisit and revise research skills such as establishing what they already know about the place, identifying research questions that they wish to answer, skimming, scanning and close reading techniques. Broaden the discussion to explore how they think that the writers and producers of the guides that they have looked at so far researched and composed their information.	
Communication: work collaboratively to come to a group decision	### Independent work In their groups, children can discuss, identify and list the key features and interesting elements of their chosen locations. Remind them to bear in mind the identified audience for, and format of, their guides. They can consider how and where they will carry out their research and, if necessary, allocate particular research to specific members of the group.	**Extend:** focus on groups who have chosen fictional or imaginary locations; how do they propose to research their locations, given they don't actually exist?
	### Plenary Ask each group to share their decisions from the independent activity with the class. Are other children able to offer suggestions and advice to support the research? Encourage the children to think about varied and effective ways of presenting the information in their guides. Again, remind the children to consider their experiences of guides so far during this Unit to support this activity.	

DAY 3 Interviewing and role play

Key features	Stages	Additional opportunities
	Introduction Remind children of their discussions and conclusions about researching their chosen location during the previous lesson. Focus attention on the intended audience for their guides. Do the children feel that their audiences can or should be consulted during the research process? Explore the feasibility of this, expanding the discussion to include the possibility of interviewing audiences remotely, for example by phone, letter, video link. Ask children who have chosen fictional or imaginary locations to think about how they might consult their audiences.	
Enquiry: seeking answers to questions	**Independent work** Groups can develop a list of questions that they want to ask the intended audience for their guides. They can also consider the social skills involved, such as seeking permission to ask questions, thanking the interviewee. Ask the groups to consider how they will record the interviews – notes, video or audio. Provide copies of photocopiable page 133 'Planning interviews' to help the children plan their interviews.	**Support:** encourage the children to consider what they specifically want to find out during the interviews and how phrasing the questions in different ways might elicit fuller responses (for example, using open-ended rather than closed questions)
Information processing: identifying relevant information	**Speaking and listening** Allow groups opportunities and time to carry out interviews. Encourage children to consider role play options, particularly for those groups who have chosen fictional or imaginary locations. **Plenary** Discuss the effectiveness of the interviews. Did the groups gather information that was useful? Ask children involved in role-play situations how this helped them to glean information, both as interviewer and interviewee.	

Guided reading
Support children in formulating questions – both for researching texts and for interviews. Demonstrate how asking interviewees open questions elicits a fuller response than asking closed questions. Involve children in role-play situations that explore asking and answering questions.

Assessment
Use discussion and role play to explore a real scenario (teacher observation and feedback from other children). Refer back to the learning outcomes on page 121.

Further work
Use further drama activities, such as hot-seating and freeze-framing, to explore participants' thoughts and emotions in real-life situations.

DAY 1 ■ Researching information

Key features	Stages	Additional opportunities
	Introduction Remind the children that they have been focusing in recent lessons on researching their chosen locations. Explore the possibilities and value of interviewing other people whose views may be useful, for example workers, residents or visitors at the location.	
	Speaking and listening Some groups can carry out further interviews – face to face, remotely or through role-play situations.	
Information processing: identify relevant information from a range of sources	**Independent work** Ask children to revisit the research questions that they developed in Day 2 of the previous Phase. Suggest that they reflect on the questions and amend or add to them accordingly. Groups can then carry out their research in order to produce information that will be included in their guides.	**Support:** work with the children during research, supporting them in identifying key words and phrases in their research questions and then scanning texts to find the answers
	Plenary Discuss the research activity with the class. Did they find any questions easier to answer than others? What were the most useful sources of information? How did their existing research skills support them in gaining information? Ask each group to reflect on the information they have found so far. Will they need to carry out further research or do they have sufficient information to start planning their guides? In the light of children's responses, allow more research time where necessary.	

DAY 2 ■ Making visual representations

Key features	Stages	Additional opportunities
	Introduction Discuss with the children the progress that they feel they have made towards gathering the information they need to produce their guides. Establish whether any groups need more time to research, and arrange when and how they will do this.	
	Independent work Ask each group to produce a map or diagram as a visual representation of their chosen location. On it they can plot interesting features that they intend to concentrate on in their guides. Suggest that they also include features that may not seem particularly interesting but would be useful, such as public toilets and restaurants. They should also mark entrances and exits. The groups can then plot a route around the location that includes as many of the features as possible.	**ICT:** support a group in producing an ICT-based visual representation of their chosen location
Communication: discuss the content of the non-fiction text they are creating	**Plenary** Ask groups to 'walk' the rest of the class around their maps, pointing out the features that they have identified as being of interest or of use. Encourage the rest of the class to offer suggestions as to how the routes can be amended or improved if necessary. Within the groups, children can allocate various features to individuals. Explain that each individual will have the responsibility for producing the section of the guide that focuses on their particular feature, in terms of visual, audio and/or written information.	

DAY 3 ■ Identifying presentational features

Key features	Stages	Additional opportunities
	### Introduction Remind the children of the combination of visual images, text and audio that they have explored in the various guide formats. Discuss how these elements combine and support each other in giving information in a way that is easily understood by the intended audience.	
Communication: working collaboratively **Reasoning:** deciding on appropriate presentational features	### Independent work Ask each group to revisit the visual representations of their chosen locations that they produced in the previous lesson. As a group, they should discuss and decide upon the presentational features that they want to include in their guides as a whole and about each interesting feature specifically. Allow the child responsible for each feature to make the ultimate decision about how their feature will be presented. Groups can then discuss the practicalities of obtaining the photographs, video, audio recordings and so on.	**Support:** work with children to identify the most effective way of presenting information and in being realistic about what they can achieve
	### Plenary Explore the presentational features that each group has decided to include – in terms of both usefulness and practicality. Discuss with the class how they can add interactive features to their guides that involve the audience. This could be in terms of questions if the guide is to be presented mainly in a written format, a picture quiz if it is going to be mainly visual or the inclusion of hyperlinks if the guide is going to be ICT-based.	

Guided reading
Work with the children on identifying the key features of their chosen locations and planning a suitable route around the location to include these features. Encourage them to visualise the location and imagine what they would want to see and do if they were visitors. Explain that putting themselves in the role of the audience can help with planning, creating and writing their guides.

Assessment
Plan effectively for a particular purpose and audience when presenting non-fiction information in a multimodal and interactive medium (self-evaluation and feedback). Refer back to the learning outcomes on page 121.

Further work
Encourage groups to try out their ideas for their guides on a potential audience or, if this is not possible, with other groups in the class. Create a supportive atmosphere of feedback and support in which children are willing to both give and receive constructive criticism.

DAY 1 ■ Planning guides

Key features	Stages	Additional opportunities
Evaluation: discuss success criteria	### Introduction Remind the children that they have been exploring guides to places. Ask them to discuss, in pairs, which of the guides that they have looked at are the most informative and effective. Encourage the children to elaborate on their responses by referring to specific examples from the guides. Based on this discussion, ask the children to consider a number of success criteria that they could use to evaluate a guide. Given that the children are going to produce guides in a variety of formats, the success criteria will need to be fairly generic. List and display the agreed success criteria. Remind the children to refer to the list as they progress through the rest of the Unit. Ask each group to tell the rest of the class the location and the audience that they have identified for their guide and to elaborate on the format that they have chosen. Ask them to explain what impact their choice of audience will have on the guide. Discuss with the class how they are going to plan their guides, drawing in the preparatory work done so far on incorporating visual elements and planning a route around the location.	**Support:** discuss with the children how to present information most effectively (for example, through the spoken word, written word or visually)
	### Independent work Give groups the opportunity to plan the content and layout of their guides. Ensure that all members of the group will be involved in the production of the guide. Give them a copy of photocopiable page 134 'Planning a guide flatplan'.	
	### Plenary Discuss the progress each group has made in planning their guide.	

DAY 2 ■ Drafting guides

Key features	Stages	Additional opportunities
	### Introduction Explain to the children that they are going to start to turn the plans that they completed in the previous lesson into draft versions of their guides. Remind the children that in Day 2 of the previous Phase they each took responsibility for particular features and that they are now going to concentrate on those features.	
Information processing: use relevant information as a basis for writing	### Independent work Individually, children can work on draft versions of the section of the guides that they have responsibility for. Once they are completed, ask the children to get together in their groups and to share their drafts. They can discuss the use they have made of visual, written and spoken elements. How well do they feel that their guides are meeting the needs of their identified audience?	**ICT:** support children in their use of ICT (for example, inserting photographs and video clips, using hyperlinks)
	### Plenary Explore the progress that the groups have made so far. Discuss with the children the fact that as they are each responsible for producing sections of the guide that focus on particular features, the 'voice' will vary throughout the guides. Explore whether the children feel that this is an issue. If they feel that it is, how will they ensure that their guide has a consistent voice? Revisit and remind the children of the success criteria produced in the previous lesson. Do the children feel that they are meeting the success criteria? If not, how do they feel they can address this?	

DAY 3 ■ Revising guides

Key features	Stages	Additional opportunities
Evaluation: evaluate the effectiveness of guides according to established success criteria	**Introduction** Discuss with the children the progress that they have made so far with their guides. Explain that they are going to have the opportunity to share their draft versions of their guides with another group. Remind the children of the success criteria that they are using to evaluate their guides. **Speaking and listening** Pair up the groups and allow them time to share their guides. You may wish to pair groups that are producing guides in similar formats. Ask the groups to ensure that they explain how they foresee the visual, spoken and written elements supporting each other. Encourage children to offer suggestions as to how the guides can be altered and improved. Promote discussion between the groups as they explore ways in which the guides can be amended. **Independent work** Ask the groups to discuss and then revise their draft guides in the light of the comments that their peers have made. **Plenary** Ask the groups to explain the changes they have made to their draft guides. Discuss with the class how giving and receiving feedback can support, or hinder, the writing process.	**Support:** work with children to develop their responses to the draft guides under the headings likes, dislikes, puzzles and patterns; explore these responses with the children

DAY 4 ■ Editing guides

Key features	Stages	Additional opportunities
Evaluation: share writing and presentations, give feedback and judge effectiveness of own work	**Introduction** Choose two or three examples of sections from the guides that have been developed so far and present them to the class. These can represent written, visual and oral forms, if available. Ask the authors of the examples to explain who the intended audience is. As a class, discuss the impact of the texts, focusing particularly on the way they are structured and the language that has been used. How do the children feel the texts can be improved? Demonstrate to the children how to edit the texts in response to their comments. Explore how the form of the texts has an impact on the audience. **Independent work** Ask the children to work individually on re-reading and editing their sections of the group guides. Once they have completed this, they can work collaboratively in their groups, putting the various sections of their guides together. Suggest to the groups that they try reading, watching or listening to their guides with fresh eyes, as if they were the target audience experiencing the guide for the first time. Does this reveal any areas that need further work? **Plenary** Explore the progress each group has made and ask them to identify what further work needs to be done on their guides before they are ready to present to the target audience. Ask each group to revisit the success criteria established at the beginning of this Phase and to consider whether they are being met.	**Support:** work with a group as a critical friend, modelling how to give and receive constructive criticism

DAY 5 ■ Completing guides

Key features	Stages	Additional opportunities
	Introduction Explain to the children that during this lesson they will be bringing their guides to publication standard.	
Communication: identify work that needs to be done and collaborate in completing a task	**Speaking and listening** Each group can discuss what work needs to be done on their guides in order to finish them. Ensure that groups delegate this work to individuals as appropriate and that they are aware of the time scale that they are working to.	
	Independent work Allow groups time to finish their guides, bringing them to an agreed level of completion.	**ICT:** support children in their use of ICT (for example, inserting photographs and video clips, using hyperlinks)
	Plenary Give each group the opportunity to present their completed guide to the rest of the class. Ask the group whether they feel that they have met the success criteria established at the beginning of the Phase. Ask the rest of the class, as the audience for each guide, to consider whether the success criteria have been achieved. Discuss with each group what they are particularly pleased with in their guides, what proved problematic and whether they had to change their plans during the production.	

DAY 6 ■ Presenting and evaluating guides

Key features	Stages	Additional opportunities
	Introduction Tell the children that in this lesson they are going to have the opportunity to present their guides to their intended audiences. Ask them to think about how they might elicit a response from the audience – for example, through asking for opinions, asking questions, evaluation forms. Discuss which of these would be appropriate and useful.	
	Speaking and listening Give each group time to prepare a relatively brief oral presentation for the identified audience that puts their guide into context. They can also decide on how they are going to gauge the response of their audience and whether this will be elicited in a formal or informal manner.	**Support:** work with groups who decide on using an evaluation form to gauge the response of the audience. Help them to develop appropriate categories for a scoring system
	Independent work Allow each group the opportunity to present their guide to the intended audience, introducing it with the prepared oral presentation and ending by taking feedback, in the agreed manner, from the audience.	
Evaluation: judge the effectiveness of the guides and the presentations	**Plenary** Take feedback from each group about the experience of presenting their guide to the audience. What was the response of the audience? Would the children change anything in their guides in the light of the audience's responses?	

Guided reading

Support children in the planning, drafting, revising and writing process. Draw children's attention, at each stage in the process, to how thinking about the audience has an impact on the way they write or present the information. Give children the opportunity of appropriate peer support when they are working on ICT aspects of their guides.

Assessment

Write or create an effective non-fiction text, making appropriate language, style and presentational choices to meet a particular purpose and audience when working in a multimodal and interactive (ICT) context (marking and feedback against agreed success criteria).
Ask children to complete the CD-ROM assessment activity 'Guides – self evaluation'.
Refer back to the learning outcomes on page 121.

Further work

Encourage groups to consider adding further interactive elements to their guides through the use of ICT. Ask them to think about any changes they would need to make if the audience for their guide was to change dramatically.

Analysing guides

■ Use this sheet to make notes about the guides you are reading, watching or listening to.

Title of the guide	Format (written, visual, audio)	Intended audience	Purpose of the guide
How information is given visually	Other ways information is given	What I like about the guide	What I dislike and how it could be improved

Planning interviews

■ Use this sheet to help you to plan your interviews.

What will the main subject of the interview be?

_____

_____

_____

_____

Who to interview – how many people?
(include whether the interviewees will have to be a specifc gender/age range)

_____

_____

_____

_____

How will the interviews take place?

☐ Face to face

☐ Telephone

How will we record the answers?

☐ Audio

☐ Video

☐ Note taking

Will questions be open/closed/ combination?

☐ Open

☐ Closed

☐ Combination

Type of questions to ask

_____

_____

_____

_____

_____

_____

_____

_____

_____

_____

Name _____   Date _____

Planning a guide flatplan

■ Use this flatplan to plan your guide if it is to be in written format. Publishers use flatplans like these to plan their publications.

Page _____

Page _____

Page _____

Page _____

Page _____

Page _____

Page _____

Page _____

Page _____

Page _____

Page _____

Page _____

100 LITERACY FRAMEWORK LESSONS YEAR 6

POETRY
UNIT 1 The power of imagery

Speak and listen for a range of purposes on paper and on screen

Strand 1 Speaking
- Use a range of oral techniques to present persuasive arguments and engaging narratives.
- Use the techniques of dialogic talk to explore ideas, topics or issues.

Strand 2 Listening and responding
- Analyse and evaluate how speakers present points effectively through use of language and gesture.

Strand 3 Group discussion and interaction
- Understand and use a variety of ways to criticise constructively and respond to criticism.

Strand 4 Drama
- Consider the overall impact of a live or recorded performance, identifying dramatic ways of conveying character's ideas and building tension.

Read for a range of purposes on paper and on screen

Strand 6 Word structure and spelling
- Use a range of appropriate strategies to edit, proofread and correct spelling in their own work, on paper and on screen.

Strand 7 Understanding and interpreting texts
- Understand underlying themes, causes and points of view.
- Understand how writers use different structures to create coherence and impact.

Strand 8 Engaging with and responding to texts
- Read extensively and discuss personal reading with others, including in reading groups.
- Compare how writers from different times and places present experiences and use language.

Write for a range of purposes on paper and on screen

Strand 9 Creating and shaping texts
- Select words and language drawing on their knowledge of literary features and formal and informal writing.

Strand 10 Text structure and organisation
- Use varied structures to shape and organise texts coherently.

Strand 12 Presentation
- Use different styles of handwriting for different purposes with a range of media, developing a consistent and personal legible style.
- Select from a wide range of ICT programs to present text effectively and communicate information and ideas.

Progression in poetry

In this year children are moving towards:
- Using language imaginatively to create surreal, surprising, amusing and inventive poetry.
- Using simple metaphors and personification to create poems based on real or imagined experience.
- Selecting pattern or form to match meaning and own voice.

▶

UNIT 1 ◄ The power of imagery *continued*

Key aspects of learning covered in this Unit

Enquiry
Children will seek answers to their own and others' questions in their reading.

Information processing
Children will explore and tease out the information communicated through the language and forms of poetry.

Evaluation
Children will share their own writing outcomes, as well as those of others. They will discuss success criteria, give feedback to others and judge the effectiveness of their own work.

Reasoning
Children will identify, explore and generate the mental connections represented within various forms of powerful imagery (simile and metaphor) – a vital aspect of thinking, reasoning and understanding.

Empathy
In discussing and writing about the poems and their images, children will need to imagine themselves in another person's position. They will explore techniques that facilitate this process.

Self-awareness
Children will discuss and reflect on their personal responses to the texts.

Communication
Children will develop their ability to discuss effective communication in respect of both the language and the content of poetry they are reading and writing. They will sometimes work collaboratively in pairs and groups. They will communicate outcomes orally, and in writing, possibly including the use of ICT.

Prior learning

Before starting this Unit check that the children can:
■ Discuss their responses to a range of poetry they have read.
■ Identify and discuss the various features of a poem, including the structure and organisation of the text and the way language is used to create an effect on the reader.
If they need further support please refer to a prior Unit or a similar Unit in Year 5.

Resources

Phase 1:
The Sea by James Reeves ❆; *The Storm* by Roger Hurn ❆; *City Jungle* by Pie Corbett ❆; Photocopiable page 145 'Personification'; *The Old House* by Roger Hurn ❆

Phase 2:
My Mum by Roger Hurn ❆; Photocopiable page 146 'Similes and metaphors'

Phase 3:
Fantastic Facts by John Irwin; *In the Land of Tir Na Nog* by Roger Hurn ❆; Photocopiable page 147 'Another world'; Interactive activity 'Another world' ❆; Photocopiable page 148 'A strange day'

Phase 4:
Assessment activity 'Imagery' ❆

Cross-curricular opportunities

Geography – topic on different lands

UNIT 1 ■ Teaching sequence

Phase	Children's objectives	Summary of activities	Learning outcomes
1	I can identify and explain the use of personification in a poem. I can write a poem that uses personification.	Exploring the use of personification in other poets' work, and using this experience as a basis for shared and independent writing of their own personification poems. ICT may be used to provide a visual or aural stimulus to develop and present the poems.	Children understand how poets can use personification to communicate with their readers. Children can write a poem that begins to use personification effectively.
2	I can identify and explain the use of powerful imagery in a poem. I can generate, and experiment with powerful imagery.	The learning processes of Phase 1 are repeated and varied, this time focusing on the use of powerful images in poetry.	Children understand how poets can use powerful images to communicate with their readers. Children can write a poem that begins to use powerful imagery effectively.
3	I can understand how to create surreal and amusing images. I can write poems that use surreal imagery. I can identify and explain what a trite or clichéd image is.	The learning processes of Phases 1 and 2 are once more repeated and varied, this time focusing on the use of surreal, surprising images in poetry.	Children understand how poets can use surreal, surprising and amusing images to communicate with their readers. Children can write a poem that begins to use surreal, surprising and amusing imagery effectively.
4	I can use pre-agreed selection criteria to assess and evaluate poems.	Outcomes from the whole Unit are shared and evaluated against pre-agreed criteria for the use of strong images, and then performed and/or published in some oral, paper or electronic form.	Children value their own poems and those of others and enjoy sharing them.

Provide copies of the objectives for the children.

DAY 1 ■ The Sea

Key features	Stages	Additional opportunities
	Introduction Tell the children that you are going to read them a poem that shows the poetic device of personification. Read them the poem *The Sea* from the CD-ROM.	**Extend:** challenge the children to find other poems that use personification
Reasoning: identify, explore and generate powerful imagery	**Speaking and listening** Ask the children what they think is meant by the word *personification*. Encourage them to give reasons, then explain the definition: *Personification is giving human qualities, feelings, action, or characteristics to inanimate (non-living) objects*. Use the following example to complement the definition: *The wind howled at me*. Encourage the children to make up some examples of their own.	
Communication: work collaboratively in pairs	**Independent work** Provide the children with copies of *The Storm* from the CD-ROM. In pairs, the children should read the poem and choose an inanimate object of their own and generate a list of human characteristics describing that object if it came to life. Then build their list into a poem.	**Extend:** mime how the inanimate objects they've chosen might move if they came to life; encourage them to make a 'soundscape' to accompany their poems
	Plenary Allow each pair to share their poems with the class. Discuss why certain images are so effective in helping to bring an inanimate object to life.	

DAY 2 ■ City Jungle

Key features	Stages	Additional opportunities
	Introduction Remind the children of the definition of personification. Tell them that they are going to use active verbs to help them write a poem that personifies nature.	
Self-awareness: reflect on personal responses	**Speaking and listening** Ask the children to give you some examples of active verbs. Then read them *City Jungle* from the CD-ROM. How many examples of active verbs can the children find in the poem? Ask them why the poet uses these active verbs. How effectively do they help create a menacing atmosphere? Now make two lists on the board: one with names of inanimate objects from nature, the other a list of action verbs. Take a word from the action verb list and match it with one of the inanimate objects. For example: *moon listens*. Now model how to expand these two words into a sentence that has power and impact. For example: *The moon listens to the stars as they sing*. Use photocopiable page 145 'Personification' and encourage the children to suggest other sentences by matching active verbs and objects from the list and then developing them.	**Extend:** challenge children to find as many examples as they can of the poet describing an object in the city as if it were a creature in the jungle; they should take examples of linking an action verb with a noun (for example, *headlights stare, motorbike snarls*) and say why they create the impression of jungle animals
Communication: work collaboratively in pairs	**Independent work** In pairs, let the children match nouns and active verbs and then discuss appropriate sentences. Ask them to select the lines that work most effectively and to make a poem that personifies the natural world.	
Evaluation: give feedback to others	**Plenary** Each pair should share their poem with the class. Allow the children to comment constructively on each other's work. Recap the definition of an active verb.	

DAY 3 ■ The Old House

Key features	Stages	Additional opportunities

Introduction
Recap on the work covered so far on personification. Tell the children that together you are going to write a personification poem.

Speaking and listening
Communication: discuss effective communication

Read *The Old House* from the CD-ROM and discuss it. Ask the children why they think Death has come to the party and invite them to describe what Death might be thinking. What might happen if one of the party goers stepped outside the old house? Select some ideas and work with the children, model writing the poem.

Independent work
Ask the children to choose a different abstract concept (such as anger, fear, happiness) and work with a partner to create their own personification poem.

Evaluation: give feedback to others

Plenary
The children should read their poems aloud. Ask the listeners to say which images they think work well and how others may be improved.

Guided reading
Ask the children what word they can see hiding inside the word *personification*. Ask them what clue that word gives to the meaning of personification. Give them some short poems. Ask the children to read them and underline all the examples of personification they can identify.

Assessment
Read a poem that shows personification. Can the class identify what is being personified and how that effect is being achieved? Refer back to the learning outcomes on page 137.

Further work
Ask the children to re-read the personification poems. Invite them to identify the different mood and tone of each poem and to describe how each poet uses personification to contribute to that mood.
Ask the children to write a short review of each poem saying why they think it is effective and how it makes them feel.

DAY 1 ■ My Mum

Key features	Stages	Additional opportunities
	### Introduction	
	Ask the children how personification is usually used in poetry – to give human qualities to non-human things. Encourage them to give examples.	**Extend:** see how many examples of giving non-human qualities to humans the children can generate; for example: *The professor's brain is a super-computer. It whirrs and flashes and beeps*
Reasoning: identify, explore and generate powerful imagery	### Speaking and listening	
	Now tell the children you are going to read them a poem that does precisely the opposite. It takes a human subject and gives that human the qualities of a machine. Read the poem *My Mum* from the CD-ROM to the class. Point out that the mum in the poem must be quite a formidable character for her child to ascribe to her the attributes of a steamroller. Ask the children to say why they think it's appropriate for the poem's narrator to personify Dad as a pancake. Invite them to suggest what type of object he would need to be to stop Mum.	
Communication: work collaboratively in pairs or groups	### Independent work	
	Put the children in pairs or small groups and have them add more machine-like qualities to Mum, such as: *Her loud voice is a foghorn, her sharp eyes blazing headlights.*	
	### Plenary	
	Allow the children to share their ideas with each other. Then extend and develop the original poem by adding the most appropriate suggestions to it.	

DAY 2 ■ Similes and metaphors

Key features	Stages	Additional opportunities
	### Introduction	
Reasoning: identify, explore and generate powerful verbs	Remind the children that normally personification uses similes and metaphors in which language relating to human behaviour, thoughts and emotions is linked to non-human things or ideas, such as *The sun smiled down on our picnic* (metaphor) or *The wind was like a giant hand pushing me backwards* (simile). Explain to the children that they will be using similes and metaphors to create powerful and appropriate images that link two unrelated things together – but that they will be reversing the usual personification process.	**Extend:** challenge the children to make a list of metaphors that juxtapose opposites; for example: *living corpses; silent scream; black light* and so on
	### Speaking and listening	
	Explain the difference between a metaphor and a simile. (For example: *Her heart was stone* – metaphor. *Her heart was like a stone* – simile.) Ask the children to give you examples of both metaphors and similes.	
	### Independent work	**Extend:** ask the children to collect familiar similes and then rewrite them to give them a fresh twist; for example, *As cold as ice* could become *as cold as a polar bear's nose*
	Put each child with a writing partner and challenge them to write some vivid metaphors and similes. For example: *I am a tiger, you are a gazelle* (metaphor). *His handshake was like wet custard* (simile). Use photocopiable page 146 'Similes and metaphors'.	
	### Plenary	
	Ask the children to read out their examples and check that they have grasped the difference between a metaphor and a simile.	

DAY 3 ■ Unpredictable twists

Key features	Stages	Additional opportunities

Introduction
Explain to the children that they are going to write a short poem that uses metaphors and similes to give their ideas unpredictable twists.

Extend: invite the children to write poems in which famous people or people they know well become types of fruit, weather, geographical features, types of music and so on

Speaking and listening

Reasoning: explore and generate powerful imagery

Write the name of a well-known person on the board and ask the children to imagine that the person has been transformed into something else, such as a musical instrument, a meal, and so on. Ask the children to say what kind of musical instrument or meal that person would be, and why. Challenge them to explain exactly in what way the person is like this. Now explain how poets use powerful images like these to communicate their ideas. Use the children's suggestions to model writing a short poem that conveys the idea of a person either as an inanimate object, an abstract concept, an animal or a plant. For example:

> My auntie's an orange
> She's round and wears fake tan
> She's sharp and sour as juice
> And she always gives me the pip.

Independent work
Invite the children to write a poem of their own in the same style.

Plenary
Ask the children to share some of their poems.

Guided writing
Tell the children that powerful imagery really brings a poem to life. Point out that imagery, however striking, is meaningless unless it serves the purpose the poet intended. For example, a poem about a crocodile may use imagery that emphasises qualities of latent danger. For example: *The crocodile, still as Sunday morning, smiles not a greeting but a warning.* Now ask the children to write examples of images that convey a sense of:
- fear
- happiness
- anger
- sadness.

Assessment
Read the children a poem with powerful imagery. Ask them to identify particularly potent images and to explain what purpose these images serve in the context of the poem.
Refer back to the learning outcomes on page 137.

Further work
Give the children pictures of various objects (fruit, animals, buildings) and ask them to write down an image for each one that sums up what they see. For example, a picture of an Old English Sheepdog might inspire the mental image of a carpet on legs, while a petrol pump might conjure up the image of a space alien with its finger in its ear. Then ask each child to take turns to read out their images. When they do, the other children should try to match the written image with the picture that inspired it.

DAY 1 ■ Fantastic Facts

Key features	Stages	Additional opportunities
	### Introduction Tell the children that poets often use surreal images and stand logic 'on its head' to create poems that surprise the reader or listener and encourage them to see familiar things in a fresh and amusing way.	**Extend:** challenge the children to make up some fantastic facts with a nautical theme. For example: *Sharks play in the park but only after dark; Whales go off the rails when they've been drinking ale; Bream will often scream when having horrid dreams*
Information processing: explore information communicated	### Speaking and listening Read the poem *Fantastic Facts* from the CD-ROM. Ask the children for their reactions to it. Does it amuse them? Why? Why is the poem called *Fantastic Facts* when nothing mentioned is actually a fact but rather a striking and unusual image? Explore which of the images is the most surprising, inventive and effective in achieving the poet's aim of making them smile.	
Communication: work collaboratively in groups	### Independent work Organise the children into groups of four. Point out that the poem *Fantastic Facts* has a geographical theme. Ask each group to write a similar fantastical poem but one that uses different countries, such as France, USA, China, Italy. Each child in the group should take one of the countries and come up with a 'fantastic fact' about it. The children then combine their ideas into one poem.	
	### Plenary Ask the groups to share their 'fantastic facts' poems with each other. Encourage the children to comment constructively on which 'facts' have the most impact and why.	

DAY 2 ■ In the Land of Tir Na Nog

Key features	Stages	Additional opportunities
	### Introduction Tell the children that you're going to read them a surreal poem called *In the Land of Tir Na Nog*. Explain that 'Tir Na Nog' is a legendary place in Celtic mythology where wonders happen and anything is possible.	**Extend:** challenge the children to find out more about the mythical world and legends of Tir Na Nog
Reasoning: identify and explore powerful imagery	### Speaking and listening Read the poem *In the Land of Tir Na Nog* from the CD-ROM. Discuss how the poet has used images to create a place that has a distinct sense of other worldliness. Ask the children to give examples from the text that turn accepted reality upside down or fly in the face of common sense. Explore the way in which the poet subverts the meaning of words, for example when 'closing down sales' are used to propel a ship. Talk about how the poet might have found himself in Tir Na Nog and the way in which writers and poets use literary devices such as magical mirrors, enchanted wardrobes and so on, to open the way into fantasy worlds. Model how the children can use these devices as springboards into writing surreal poetry.	**Extend:** ask the children to write an extended poem describing an adventure in Tir Na Nog.
	### Independent work Give each child a copy of photocopiable page 147 'Another world' and ask them to complete the poem by either choosing words from the list on the frame or by adding their own words. Or children could complete the interactive version from the CD-ROM.	**Extend:** encourage the children to read stories set in surreal or 'other' worlds, such as *Alice's Adventures in Wonderland* or *The Wizard of Oz*
	### Plenary Ask the children to read out their favourite images from the completed poems. Discuss which images are the most effective and why.	

DAY 3 ■ Surreal imagery

Key features	Stages	Additional opportunities
	### Introduction	

Information processing: explore information communicated through poetry

Communication: work collaboratively in pairs

Introduction
Tell the children that together you are going to create some weird and wacky poems that make use of surreal imagery.

Speaking and listening
Hold a brainstorming session and challenge the children to come up with bizarre similes and metaphors as well as surprising ideas and word combinations. For example: *as cold as the sun at midnight; as hot as chilli-flavoured icicles.* Encourage them to play with the language they've created in order to subvert the expectations of the listener/reader. For example, take the traditional notion that kissing a frog will turn it into a prince and then reverse it: *The prince, handsome as a handbag but stupid as a log, kissed his own reflection and turned into a frog.*

Independent work
Either individually, or in pairs, set the children the task of writing a poem called *A Strange Day*. The poem should be a collection of curious and unusual images, similes and metaphors that together create a vision of a day that is totally out of the ordinary. Some children may be able to do this unaided but others may benefit from using photocopiable page 148 'A Strange Day'.

Plenary
Read the poems together. Discuss why putting unlikely ideas together helps give a fresh perspective and impetus to descriptive language.

Extend: ask the children to make weird and wacky nonsense poems by cutting out lines from different articles in magazines and sticking them together at random on a sheet of plain paper

Guided reading
Explain to the children that if something is 'surreal' it is fantastical, unbelievable and has the intensely irrational qualities of a dream. Ask the children to write about an actual dream they have had where weird things happened.

Assessment
Display this definition of a cliché: *A cliché is an expression that has been used so often that its original power has been drained away.*
Ask the children to give examples of clichés. (As good as gold, big as a house...) Now ask them to give alternative and livelier expressions that could replace clichés. For example: *as nervous as a kitten* becomes *as nervous as a long tailed cat in a room full of rocking chairs.* Refer back to the learning outcomes on page 137.

Further work
Ask the children to find more surreal poems – for example, *Jabberwocky, The Owl and the Pussy Cat.* Put them in pairs and invite them to write and illustrate their own versions of these dreamlike poems.

DAY 1 ■ 'The colour blue tastes like cold rice pudding'

Key features	Stages	Additional opportunities
	### Introduction Tell the children that they are going to read through all the poems they have created so far and then select the ones they think make the most striking, powerful and original use of imagery for use in a class anthology of poetry.	
	### Speaking and listening Help the children make informed decisions as to the quality of their poems by reminding them that poetry makes the most creative use of language possible by combining words and ideas together in ways that might seem nonsensical, inappropriate or even wrong. Point out that, if done well, this helps their poems give voice to new and more vivid forms of expression. For example: *The colour blue tastes like cold rice pudding.* Explain that their poems don't have to rhyme but they must avoid clichés, explore ideas in a fresh way and have an effect on their audience.	**ICT:** let the children make a computer presentation of the chosen poems
Evaluation: discuss success criteria and give feedback to others	### Independent work Let the children revisit their poems. Ask them to work with partners to review, revise and edit each others' poems. Now invite each child to choose one of their partner's poems that they feel best meets the selection criteria for the anthology.	**Extend:** invite the children to visit The Poetry Zone (www.poetryzone.ndirect.co.uk/index2.htm) and publish their poems online
	### Plenary Ask each child to read out the poem that they particularly liked. Let them give reasons why they feel it should be included in the class anthology. Find some praiseworthy aspect in every child's contribution. Collect the chosen poems and publish them in the class anthology.	

Guided writing

Explain that it is very rare for a poet to write a poem in one go and be completely happy with it, so that's why redrafting is important. Ask the children to redraft their poems using the following criteria:

■ the second draft should not be the same as the first draft only neater;

■ the title should fit what's written in the poem;

■ not all words are necessary so, if the poem works without certain words, cut them out;

■ if a phrase is tired or clichéd, change it.

Assessment

Ask the children to make a list of all the qualities they think go to make up a good poem, such as an interesting subject, dramatic imagery, a clear structure, originality and so on. Discuss their lists with them. Are there any glaring omissions? Ask them to use their list as an assessment tool and apply it to the poems they have written. How far do their own poems meet their criteria? Ask the children to complete the CD-ROM assessment activity 'Imagery'. Refer back to the learning outcomes on page 137.

Further work

The children could organise and give a series of poetry readings for younger children.

Name _____ Date _____

Personification

Inanimate objects

moon, grass, clouds, wind, flowers, stars, rocks, sun, mountain

■ Can you list some more objects?

_____

_____

_____

_____

_____

Action verbs

listen, whisper, blow, howl, sway, sing, cry, push, laugh, cackle

■ Can you list some more action verbs?

_____

_____

_____

_____

_____

■ Take a word from the action verb list and match it with one of the inanimate objects, expand these words into sentences below.

_____

_____

_____

_____

_____

_____

_____

_____

Name _____   Date _____

Similes and metaphors

■ Complete these similes.

His face was like _____

His handshake was _____

Her voice was _____

She cried like _____

My brother danced like _____

My uncle shouted like _____

My aunty laughed like _____

The sun was like _____

The moon was like _____

■ Make up some metaphors using the words below and then use them in appropriate
sentences, for example:

As fury surged through my veins I became a tiger in defence of my friend.

> tiger, tree, bird, sky, stars, sea, tower, road, bridge, snake, jewels, stone, dirt, earth,
> compass, clock, sun, moon, ball, stars, carpet, rug, mountains, rock, aeroplane, car,
> train, railtrack, river, beach, shells, elephant, cat, night, day, dusk, dawn, rain, thunder,
> sunshine, breeze, grass, lawn, house, diamond

_____

_____

_____

_____

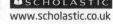

Name _____ Date _____

Another world

■ Complete this poem. You may want to fill in the gaps with words of your own or you may
want to use some of the words in the box below.

I fell through a _____ on my way to school

And found myself in a land that was full of _____

Some of them were _____ and some of them were _____

A few of them were _____ but most of them were _____

I saw _____ shimmering in the murky _____

While _____ played blind man's bluff with _____

I don't think I was _____ but it's so hard to _____

For nothing is quite what it seems in the land called _____

blots, rubbery, dreaming, sky, green, red, mirror, stars, tiny tots, window, custard pies, roses, say, ridiculous, pomegranates, lead, clean, toads, doorway, rules, resilient, fools, park, mules, manhole, brilliant, evil, dark, jewels, know, shrubbery, teapots, not so far, centipedes, air, fried eggs, steel guitars, octopods, noses, wishing well, planets, tic tac toe

Illustration © Nova Developments.

Name _____   Date _____

A strange day

(Poetry frame)

■ Complete this poem using similes and metaphors to create unusual images.

It was a strange day.

The sun was as cold as _____

The sky was _____

I felt like a _____

I saw a _____

I heard a _____

I thought I was _____

It was a strange day.

POETRY
UNIT 2 Finding a voice

Speak and listen for a range of purposes on paper and on screen

Strand 1 Speaking
- Use a range of oral techniques to present persuasive arguments and engaging narratives.
- Participate in whole-class debate using the conventions and language of debate, including standard English.
- Use the techniques of dialogic talk to explore ideas, topics or issues.

Strand 2 Listening and responding
- Analyse and evaluate how speakers present points effectively through use of language and gesture.
- Identify the way spoken language varies according to differences in context and purpose of use.

Strand 3 Group discussion and interaction
- Understand and use a variety of ways to criticise constructively and respond to criticism.

Strand 4 Drama
- Improvise using a range of drama strategies and conventions to explore themes such as hopes, fears and desires.
- Consider the overall impact of a live or recorded performance, identifying dramatic ways of conveying characters' ideas and building tension.

Read for a range of purposes on paper and on screen

Strand 6 Word structure and spelling
- Use a range of appropriate strategies to edit, proofread and correct spelling in own work, on paper and on screen.

Strand 7 Understanding and interpreting texts
- Understand underlying themes, causes and points of view.
- Understand how writers use different structures to create coherence and impact.

Strand 8 Engaging with and responding to texts
- Read extensively and discuss personal reading with others.
- Compare how writers from different times and places present experiences and use language.

Write for a range of purposes on paper and on screen

Strand 9 Creating and shaping texts
- Select words and language drawing on their knowledge of literary features and formal and informal writing

Strand 10 Text structure and organisation
- Use varied structures to shape and organise text coherently

Strand 12 Presentation
- Use different styles of handwriting for different purposes with a range of media, developing a consistent and personal legible style.

Progression in poetry

In this year children are moving towards:
- Exploring an issue meaningful to them, and at the same time reading, responding, analysing and evaluating a range of poems about that issue.

UNIT 2 ◄ Finding a voice *continued*

- Writing their own poems in response to the issue.
- Sharing and evaluating the outcomes from the whole Unit against pre-agreed criteria for effective communication with the reader.

Key aspects of learning covered in this Unit

Enquiry
The children will seek the answers to their own and others' questions in their reading.

Information processing
The children will explore and tease out the information communicated through the language of poetry.

Evaluation
Children will share their own writing outcomes, as well as those of others. They will discuss success criteria, give feedback to others and judge the effectiveness of their own work.

Reasoning
Children will identify, explore and generate the mental connections represented within the various forms of powerful imagery (simile and metaphor) – a vital aspect of thinking, reasoning and understanding.

Empathy
In discussing and writing about the poems and their images, children will need to imagine themselves in another person's position. They will explore techniques that facilitate this process.

Self-awareness
Children will discuss and reflect on their personal responses to the texts.

Communication
Children will develop their ability to discuss effective communication in respect of both the language and the content of poetry they are reading and writing. They will sometimes work collaboratively in pairs and groups. They will communicate outcomes orally, and in writing.

Prior learning

Before starting this Unit check that the children can:
- Discuss their responses to a range of poetry they have read.
- Identify and discuss the various features of a poem.

If they need further support please refer to a prior Unit or a similar Unit in Year 5.

Resources

Phase 1:
To a Fur Scarf by F.F. Van de Water ❦; Photocopiable page 158 'Discussion writing frame'; *Blake's Tyger – revisited* by Michaela Morgan ❦

Phase 2:
The Dancing Bear by Roger Hurt ❦; Dancing bear image ❦; Photocopiable page 159 'Class poem writing frame'

Phase 3:
Photocopiable page 160 'Poetry evaluation sheet'; Assessment activity 'Is it a simile or a metaphor?' ❦

Cross-curricular opportunities

PSHE

UNIT 2 ■ Teaching sequence

Phase	Children's objectives	Summary of activities	Learning outcomes
1	I can explore a meaningful issue. I can read, respond, analyse and evaluate a range of poems about that issue. I can write my own poem in response to the issue. I can share and evaluate outcomes from this Unit against pre-agreed criteria. I can perform and publish my poems.	Discussion and debate on the ethical treatment of animals by reading and responding to poems that highlight this issue. Dramatic techniques such as hot-seating, role play and conscience alley to encourage insight and understanding. Writing frames will help them construct balanced arguments.	Children understand how writers can use poetry as a powerful way of communicating their thoughts and feelings about a particular issue.
2	I can model a writing process. I can respond appropriately and effectively to a stimulus for discussion and writing. I can write an issue-based poem. I can give feedback in a constructive way. I can read my poem to an audience of my peers.	Modelling a writing process based on the stimulus of digital images and a linked poem. Responses and ideas adapted and refined. The aptness of the language and its fitness for purpose will be discussed and evaluated.	Children can write a poem that begins to use language and form effectively and powerfully to communicate to a reader their thoughts and feelings about a particular issue.
3	I can evaluate and self-evaluate poems against agreed criteria. I can learn performance and delivery techniques. I can perform a poem to an audience.	The children will evaluate and self-evaluate the poems written in the Unit against agreed criteria, with particular reference to the effectiveness of the language and imagery in communicating the writer's thoughts and feelings powerfully to the reader. They will select, organise, perform and publish some of their poems.	Children value their own poems and those of others and enjoy sharing them.

Provide copies of the objectives for the children.

DAY 1 ◼ To a Fur Scarf

Key features	Stages	Additional opportunities
Information processing: explore information communicated	**Introduction** Ask the children if they think it is right to hunt and trap animals. Take their views then tell the children you are going to read a poem written many years ago but which still has a very powerful message about trapping animals relevant today.	
Reasoning: identify and explore powerful images	**Speaking and listening** Read the poem *To a Fur Scarf* from the CD-ROM. Encourage the children to give their responses to it. Discuss the meaning of any words that may be unfamiliar and how the poet uses language to create an emotional impact. Why has the writer called the poem *To a Fur Scarf* when he is writing about the protracted death of a trapped animal? Invite the children to consider whether the killing of animals in the manner described has ethical implications for the fashion industry.	**Extend:** let the children research attitudes held by various groups towards wearing fur; for example, they could use the internet to visit sites such as www.britishfur.co.uk
Self-awareness: reflect on response to text	**Independent work** Give the children copies of photocopiable page 158 'Discussion writing frame'. Ask them to list the points for and against the wearing of animal fur and to decide their own views.	
	Plenary Ask the children to feedback on their views.	

DAY 2 ◼ Another point of view

Key features	Stages	Additional opportunities
	Introduction Remind the class of the poem *To a Fur Scarf*. Read it to them again.	
Empathy: imagine themselves in another person's position **Self-awareness:** reflect on responses to text	**Speaking and listening** Ask the children to suggest who they think is the *cruel biped*, and who is the one who set *the timid spirit free*. Encourage them to give reasons for their answers. Now invite the class to hot-seat you as the *cruel biped* who set the steel trap and answer questions as to your motives. Continue the hot-seating by taking on the role of the *One*. Encourage the children to explore why this character freed the animal's spirit. Put the children into small groups with one child from each in the hot-seat role of the trapped animal.	**Extend:** ask children to investigate the various positions held on the right of animals to be treated humanely by visiting www.bbc. co.uk/religion/ethics/ animals/rights/ positions_3.shtml
	Plenary Each group should report back to the class about the thoughts and feelings that the poem has engendered in them. Encourage the children to explore their emotional and intellectual responses to all the issues raised.	

DAY 3 ■ Animals in captivity

Key features	Stages	Additional opportunities
Enquiry: seek answers to questions **Self-awareness:** reflect on responses to text	**Introduction** Tell the children that you are now switching the focus from hunting animals for their fur to keeping wild animals in captivity. **Speaking and listening** Display the poem *Blake's Tyger – revisited* and read it with the class. Tell them that this poem was written after the poet discovered that tigers in captivity lose their beautiful colour and markings and their fur gradually fades to white. Highlight lines from the poem that suggest that the captive tiger's spirit is fading. Ask the children to consider whether zoos are good things. **Plenary** Let the children debate the issue of keeping animals in zoos – for and against. Model how to summarise their arguments.	**Extend:** ask children to read Blake's original *Tiger* poem

DAY 4 ■ Trapped

Key features	Stages	Additional opportunities
Empathy: imagine themselves in another person's position **Self-awareness:** reflect on responses to text	**Introduction** Tell the children that you would like them to try to see the world through the eyes of the animals in the two poems, *To a Fur Scarf* and *Blake's Tyger – revisited*. **Speaking and listening** Ask the children to suggest what thoughts and feelings the two trapped animals in the poems might have had. List these ideas on the board. Now ask them to explain which animal they feel most sorry for, and why. How have the poets communicated their anger at the plight of the animals? Ask the children to imagine that they are either the animal in the steel trap or the tiger in the cage and to write a few lines articulating what it felt like to be that animal. **Plenary** Encourage the children to share their writing with each other.	**Extend:** play 'conscience alley'; have two lines facing each other; one child, the hunter, walks down the alley as the others speak the thoughts that support their point of view: should he hunt or should he stop? At the end of the alley the child explains what he/she is going to do

Guided writing
In the light of the discussions they have had concerning the relationship between humans and animals, ask the children to write down arguments both for and against hunting.

Assessment
Can the children empathise with the predicament of the animals?
Ask the class to show how the poem communicates the writer's feelings on the subject.
Refer back to the learning outcomes on page 151.

Further work
Ask the children to collect a range of pictures, photos, video clips, articles and newspaper cuttings about the issue of the ethical treatment of animals.
They could create a class display on the subject.

DAY 1 ■ The Dancing Bear

Key features	Stages	Additional opportunities
	Introduction Explain to the class that you will be investigating how animals can be exploited for the purposes of entertainment.	
	Speaking and listening Read the poem *The Dancing Bear*. Discuss the feelings the narrator in the poem had when he first saw the bear in the cage and how he reacted when he saw the bear dance. List the children's responses. Ask them if they can offer any reasons as to why the narrator went back to watch the 'dance' and why he *crept away* without trying to stop the 'entertainment'.	**Extend:** children can research both sides of the argument about using animals in the entertainment industry; ask them to make a multimedia presentation to stimulate further discussion of the issue
Empathy: imagine themselves in another person's position	**Independent work** Organise the children into small groups and invite them to hot-seat each other in the role of the bear to explore how it felt about being made to perform for the crowd. People 'dance for joy', so why was it not joyful?	
	Plenary Discuss with the class whether it is right that humans use animals for the purposes of entertainment. Is it always wrong or is it acceptable to train animals for use in shows and films? Do some animals enjoy performing?	

DAY 2 ■ Responding to images

Key features	Stages	Additional opportunities
	Introduction Explain that you are going to show two rather distressing images. Say that the images will provide the stimulus for a class poem.	
Self-awareness: reflect on responses	**Speaking and listening** Now show the digital image of the dancing bear from the CD-ROM. Capture the impact made on the children by annotating the pictures with powerful words, phrases and verbal images. Ask the children to describe the thoughts and feelings these images inspire in them and to think about how they can translate their emotional responses into powerful language for a poem that will communicate directly to an audience.	**Extend:** the children could recreate the scene where the bear is made to dance; they could make their own music by using percussion instruments
Communication: work collaboratively in a group	**Independent work** Working in groups, with photocopiable page 159 'Class poem writing frame', the children should discuss and decide what it is that they want the poem to say.	
	Plenary A spokesperson for each group should report back on the outcomes of their discussions. Synthesise their responses and agree together what it is they want the class poem to say.	

DAY 3 ◾ Creating a poem

Key features	Stages	Additional opportunities
	Introduction Tell the class you are going to model writing their class poem.	**Extend:** let children set their class poem to music they have composed. Alternatively, they could provide a rhythmic accompaniment using sound effects and simple percussion while performing the poem to an audience
Communication: work collaboratively	**Speaking and listening** Revisit the list of the words, phrases and images the children volunteered after seeing the digital image of the captive bear. Remind them what they wanted the poem to say. You are going to focus on writing a free form poem that concentrates on the power of the words and verbal images chosen to convey its meaning to the reader. Work together with the class to develop the poem. Evaluate the emerging poem by reading it aloud. Let the children perform it to each other so they can assess how effective it is.	
Evaluation: share outcomes	**Plenary** Discuss the children's feedback with them and incorporate any pertinent ideas into the poem.	

DAY 4 ◾ The important issues

Key features	Stages	Additional opportunities
	Introduction Tell the children that they are going to work with a response partner to select an image about an issue that is important to them and then use it as a stimulus to write a poem about that issue.	**Extend:** children could write a series of short poems on a variety of emotive or contentious issues
	Speaking and listening Briefly recap the process of how to create a powerful piece of writing. Remind the children that poetry is about sharing an experience or strong feelings with the reader. Effective poems combine the sound, rhythm and meaning of language to create something that moves the reader and stirs their emotions. Explain that if the children succeed in doing this then their poems will have achieved their purpose. Ask the children to choose their stimulus and write their poems. Encourage them to bounce ideas off one another.	
Evaluation: give feedback to others	**Plenary** Invite the children to share some of their poems-in-progress with each other. Ask them to evaluate the poems in terms of their emotional impact and how well they communicate what the writer wanted to say.	

Guided reading
Read the class a poem that addresses a major issue. Can the children predict what the issue is? Ask them to write a poem that offers a solution to the concerns raised.

Assessment
Observe the children as they read and respond to each other's poems. Are their poems constructed using appropriate poetic devices like imagery, personification, metaphors and similes to deliver a powerful message?
Refer back to the learning outcomes on page 151.

Further work
Read the children a poem that examines a serious issue in a humorous way, such as Benjamin Zephaniah's *Talking Turkeys*. Discuss using humour to make an important point. Ask the children to write a short poem of their own that uses humour in this way.

DAY 1 ■ What makes a good poem?

Key features	Stages	Additional opportunities
	Introduction Tell the children that together you and they are going to agree a set of evaluation criteria to help them assess the quality of the poems that they have written.	
	Speaking and listening Discuss with the children the kind of things that make a good poem. For example, it should convey its meaning through vivid images and use strong, accurate, interesting and apt words that grip the reader's attention and help them feel the poet's emotions and intentions. Now discuss with the children what the evaluation criteria for their own poems should include. Remind them that good evaluation should always include pointers on how to improve the work being assessed. Write their suggestions on the board. Use these as the basis for a poetry evaluation sheet.	
Evaluation: judge effectiveness of own work	**Independent work** Put the children in pairs and ask them to apply the evaluation criteria to the poems they have written. (You may wish them to use photocopiable page 160 'Poetry evaluation sheet'.) Allow them to revise and improve their poems in the light of this assessment.	**Extend:** give the children a range of published poems and encourage them to critically evaluate these
	Plenary Discuss the importance correct spelling and punctuation can have in communicating meaning accurately.	

DAY 2 ■ Performance poetry

Key features	Stages	Additional opportunities
	Introduction Explain that in this session you are going to hold a performance poetry event.	**Extend:** encourage children to perform their poems to a wider audience
	Speaking and listening Discuss delivery techniques with the class, such as speed of delivery, tone and volume of voice, facial expressions, appropriate gestures, stance, posture, eye contact. List them on the board. Model how to perform a poem. Invite the children to give constructive feedback on your performance. Invite individual children to perform their poems. Focus on how, by applying simple techniques, they can really bring their poems to life. Display a poem and annotate it with instructions on how to deliver key words or lines, such as *say in a spooky voice* or *shake fist*.	
Evaluation: give feedback to others	**Independent work** Allow the children to read their poems silently and then ask them to make notes on how they can most effectively perform their chosen poem. They can record and listen to their poems to see if they can improve their presentation. They can practise reciting their poems to a partner or small group in order to gain confidence and refine techniques that will enable them to deliver their poems with maximum impact. The group should give constructive feedback.	**Extend:** children could publish their poems in an anthology, on the internet or in a school newspaper or magazine
	Plenary Stress the importance of active and empathetic listening, then invite the children to perform their poems to the class.	

Name _____ Date _____

Class poem writing frame

◼ Use this writing frame to jot down what your group wants the class poem to say to its readers.

◼ Make brief points under each heading explaining why this particular feeling is, or isn't, appropriate in terms of what it is that you are trying to communicate.

Our class poem should communicate our
Anger
Disgust
Amusement
Sadness
Indifference
Excitement
Outrage
Curiosity
Sympathy
Our conclusion We feel that the class poem should

Poetry evaluation sheet

■ Fill in the evaluation sections below by giving examples and as much detail as possible.

Poem title:	
How effectively does the poem use language and imagery? Does the poem use predictable language and clichés? Give examples.	
Does the poem use similes and metaphors? Are they accurate? Do they bring the poem to life? Give examples.	
Are all the words in the poem spelled correctly?	
Can you understand the meaning and purpose of the poem? Please give details.	
How effectively does the poem communicate the writer's thoughts? Give examples.	
How effectively did the poem communicate the writer's feelings? Give examples.	
What did you like most about this poem?	
What suggestions would you make to help improve this poem?	

REVISION
Unit 1 Narrative

This Unit is specifically designed to revisit and revise the reading and writing of fiction and the coverage of objectives in the Narrative section of this book. It is probably best placed in the late spring or early summer of Year 6, prior to the National Curriculum tests.

Key aspects of learning covered in this Unit

Enquiry
Children will seek out the answers to their own and others' questions in their reading.

Information processing
Children will explore and tease out information communicated through fiction texts. They will identify relevant information and use this to answer questions at literal, deductive and inferential levels.

Evaluation
Children will share their own answers and writing outcomes, as well as those of others. They will discuss success criteria, give feedback to others and judge the effectiveness of their own work.

Reasoning
To fill the requirements of some questions, children will construct reasoned arguments based on available information and evidence.

Self-awareness
Children will discuss and reflect on their personal responses to the texts.

Empathy
In discussing and writing about the books or stories, children will need to imagine themselves in another person's position. They will explore techniques that facilitate this process.

Communication
Children will develop the ability to discuss effective communication in respect of both the form and the content of the fiction texts they are reading and writing. They will sometimes work collaboratively in pairs and groups. They will communicate outcomes orally and in writing.

Prior learning

Before starting this Unit check that the children can:
■ Discuss their responses to a range of fictional or imaginative texts they have read.
■ Identify and discuss the various features of a narrative or play text, including characters, settings, themes and dilemmas, the author's intentions, the structure and organisation of the text and the way language is used to create effects on the reader
■ Employ these in their own writing as appropriate.
■ Write a variety of sentences (including compound sentences), punctuate them correctly and use them appropriately in their writing.
■ Where appropriate, organise their writing into meaningful cohesive paragraphs.
If they need further support please refer to a prior Unit or a similar Unit in Year 5.

▶

Resources

Phase 1:

The Wild Wood from *Wind in the Willows* by Kenneth Grahame ❀; Photocopiable page 169 'Types of question'; Photocopiable page 170 'The Wild Wood – test questions'; *Gibbons and ghosts* from *Kensuke's Kingdom* by Michael Morpurgo ❀; *Lady Naga* from *A Darkling Plain* by Philip Reeve ❀; Photocopiable page 171 'Lady Naga – test questions'; *Battle of Britain* from *My Story: Battle of Britain: Harry Woods* by Chris Priestly ❀; Photocopiable page 172 'Battle of Britain – test questions'

Phase 2:

A collection of fiction books; A short story collection

Cross-curricular opportunities

Extracts can be related to cross-curricular topics. However, the focus in this Unit is on revising and consolidating previously learned material, rather than new learning.

Key features	Stages	Additional opportunities
Self-awareness: reflect on personal responses to text	**Introduction** Display *The Wild Wood* from the CD-ROM. Read the passage aloud. Ask children to jot down their first responses and share these without comment (this encourages participation). Check unknown vocabulary, find definitions and check that children understand the words in the context of the passage.	**Vocabulary extension:** synonym work – malice, hatred, animosity, malevolence, spite; revise similes; revise onomatopoeia
Empathy: imagine themselves in another person's position	**Speaking and listening** In small groups, ask children to highlight and annotate the text to show how suspense is built. Encourage them to think about the literary devices used, the length of sentences and the role of punctuation. Ask the children how they think Mole felt and whether his feelings change during this extract. Prompt children to find evidence to support their opinions.	
	Independent work Ask the children to write a paragraph describing how Kenneth Grahame builds suspense in this passage.	**Extend:** write a short suspense paragraph entitled 'Lost at the seaside'
Evaluation: give feedback to others	**Plenary** Invite children to share their writing and evaluate each other's work: ■ Did they provide evidence for their ideas? ■ Did they use a range of techniques to build suspense? ■ Did they demonstrate their understanding of Mole's feelings and predicament?	

DAY 2 ■ Narrative texts: answering questions (1)

Key features	Stages	Additional opportunities
	Introduction Explain that in the SATs children will be asked different types of questions about texts. Show that some questions have more than one mark. Explain that this is because there are several pieces of information to be found or it is a more complicated question that requires them to analyse the language, give an opinion or justify an answer by providing evidence from the text. Display photocopiable page 169 'Types of question'. Explain how each type of question works and talk through the examples.	
Enquiry: seek the answers to questions in reading	**Speaking and listening** Display *The Wild Wood* extract from the CD-ROM and work through some different types of question orally, guiding children to think carefully about what the question is asking. Ask them to: *Find one simile in the passage. Describe the effect created by that simile. Find two words that tell the reader that the faces staring out from the trees were not friendly. What time of day is it when Mole enters the Wild Wood?*	
	Independent work Allow ten minutes for the children to independently answer the questions from photocopiable page 170 'The Wild Wood – test questions' about the passage. Remind children to answer the question according to the instructions.	
	Plenary Share answers to the questions. Reinforce the idea that there are a range of different types of question by asking children to identify exactly what the question is asking.	

DAY 3 ■ Narrative texts: asking questions (2)

Key features	Stages	Additional opportunities
Empathy: imagine themselves in another person's position **Enquiry:** seek out answers to questions in reading	**Introduction** Display the extract *Gibbons and ghosts* from the CD-ROM and explain that this lesson is about children generating their own questions and that going through this process can help them to think more carefully about reading questions. Read the extract. Discuss the difference between a first and third person narration. Ask the children who is telling the story. Remind them that in first person narratives the person narrating the story refers to themselves as *I*. Tell the children that in this type of story we have access to the narrator's thoughts and feelings. What is the narrator of this story thinking and feeling? **Independent work** In pairs, ask the children to write some questions that could be asked about the passage. Challenge them to write at least one question that requires: extracting information from the text; analysis of the author's language; an opinion; deduction supported by evidence. Collect all of the questions and classify them. List the five most common questions. Children can answer these questions independently or as a plenary activity. **Plenary** Review the work that has been done on children generating questions. Make explicit what they have learned and how they can apply this to answering test questions.	

DAY 4 ■ Revision: reading the comprehension paper (1)

Key features	Stages	Additional opportunities
	Introduction Summarise what has been learned about answering reading comprehension questions. Explain that today's lesson will provide an opportunity for them to practise test style questions. Points to cover: ■ Read the questions/instructions quickly and carefully. ■ Read the text and annotate it as you read. ■ Make sure you know exactly what the questions are asking. ■ Work through each question steadily. Only omit questions if you are stuck and spending too long trying to answer them. **Test practice** Provide copies of the extract *Lady Naga* from the CD-ROM and accompanying questions on photocopiable page 171. Implement the test under SATs conditions. Give the children a time limit.	

DAY 5 ▪ Revision: reading the comprehension paper (2)

Key features	Stages	Additional opportunities

Introduction

Repeat the previous day's lesson. Explain that today's lesson will provide an opportunity for them to practise test style questions. Points to cover:

■ Read the questions/instructions quickly and carefully

■ Read the text and annotate it as you read

■ Make sure you know exactly what the questions are asking

■ Work through each question steadily. Only omit questions if you are stuck and spending too long trying to answer them.

Remind children to analyse exactly what a question is asking, taking particular note of multiple choice questions. Advise children to work through the questions steadily and systematically because the questions are designed to develop a cumulative understanding. However, they should not waste time if a particular question is causing some difficulty.

Test practice

Provide copies of the extract *Battle of Britain* from the CD-ROM and accompanying questions on photocopiable page 172. Implement the test under SATs conditions. Give the children a time limit.

DAY 1 ■ Playing with sentences: connectives

Key features	Stages	Additional opportunities

Introduction
Remind the class that connectives are used to help 'stick' text together by making links to what has gone before. This gives the writing rhythm and makes it easier to understand. Tell the children that connectives can be words, for example, *next, then, after* or phrases, for example, *sometime later, it was thus that.* List some purposes of connectives found in narrative texts on the board and invite examples from the children.
- Addition – also, and, as well as.
- Opposition – however, instead, but.
- Reinforcing – anyway, after all.
- Listing – first of all.
- Indicating time:
  - Subsequent – eventually, tomorrow.
  - Prior – earlier, yesterday.
  - Concurrent – meanwhile, today.

Share some examples from fiction extracts that have been used in previous lessons and discuss the types of connectives used.

Support: prepare a short cloze passage with the connectives deleted; model how to identify appropriate connectives taking suggestions from the children

Communication: communicate outcomes in writing

Independent work
Distribute a collection of fiction books and ask children to find examples of sentences with connectives and record them.

Extend: in pairs, use a thesaurus to find synonyms for connectives; make a connectives poster for the classroom to be used as a prompt for writing

Plenary
Remind children that using the right connectives in their writing is important to ensure that the work flows and is easy to read.

DAY 2 ■ Simple, compound, complex sentences

Key features	Stages	Additional opportunities

Introduction
Ask for an example of a simple sentence (*It was a windy day.*); a compound sentence (*It was a windy day* **and** *Mrs Brown's hat blew away.*); and a complex sentence (*Mrs Brown, who was wearing a bright red hat, was almost blown off her feet by the gale-force wind.*)

Speaking and listening
Write: *The wind blew the trees, which were bent with the weight of the apples, and the branches and the leaves shook wildly.* Ask the children what they notice about the structure of this sentence. List and extend their ideas:
- It is a complex sentence.
- The sentence has an embedded subordinate clause.
- The subordinate clause does not make sense on its own. The main clause however could be read on its own.
- The subordinate clause is separated from the main clause by commas.
- The subordinate clause begins with a subordinator – *which.*

In pairs, ask the children to see if they can re-order this sentence using the same words. They should not add words but they may need to change verb endings. List suggestions. Reflect on the different effects created by moving the sentence around. Which is most effective? Why?

Communication: communicate outcomes orally

Plenary
Ask children to share examples from their own work where they would make changes to the types of sentences used. Prompt them to give reasons.

DAY 3 ▪ Revising punctuation

Key features	Stages	Additional opportunities
	Introduction Write on the board this famous opening from Charles Dickens's *Great Expectations*: *It was the best of times it was the worst of times* and ask the children to punctuate it. (It could be punctuated simply as two sentences or as one sentence *It was the best of times and it was the worst of times.*) Tell the children that Charles Dickens chose instead to link both clauses with a semicolon. *It was the best of times; it was the worst of times.* Explain to the children that it makes the connection between the two clauses stronger and more explicit than writing two separate sentences. It is also more punchy and rhythmic than the compound sentence. Here the semicolon is an unspoken connective.	**Punctuation:** at this point you may want to look at examples from Lynne Truss', *Eat Shoots and Leaves*, if you have a copy; this illustrates how poor comma use can completely alter the meaning of a sentence
Communication: work collaboratively in pairs	**Speaking and listening** In pairs, ask the children to choose a fiction book then to find all the different forms of punctuation that can be found on a random page. Ask them to come up with rules to describe how these punctuation marks are used. Take feedback and list what they find on the board.	
	Independent work Prepare a passage of fiction and replace the punctuation by a code. In pairs, ask children to work out which punctuation mark each of the symbols represents.	**Support:** prepare a passage with the punctuation removed and ask the children to add the punctuation
	Plenary Share the results of the investigations and clarify understanding. Summarise the uses of the more complex punctuation marks.	

DAY 4 ▪ Playing with paragraphs

Key features	Stages	Additional opportunities
	Introduction Choose a story that all the children know in order to demonstrate the progression of paragraphs through an entire story. For example, the story of Cinderella might be told in nine paragraphs. Invite suggestions from the Children. This could be done as a paired activity with feedback to the class. 1. Cinderella lives with her step family and is forced to live a life of drudgery. 2. A ball is announced . 3. The stepsisters prepare to attend, while Cinderella remains behind. 4. A fairy godmother arrives and transforms Cinderella. 5. At the ball she dances with the prince. 6. At midnight she leaves in a hurry and everything is changed back to normal except the glass slipper that the prince finds. 7. He searches for the owner of the slipper. 8. Cinderella's foot fits the slipper. 9. Happy ever after.	
	Independent work Distribute short story collections to small groups and ask children to discuss and analyse the way paragraphs are used in those stories.	
Communication: communicate outcomes orally	**Plenary** Share and evaluate examples. Consider the way paragraphs have been used but also reinforce previous learning about the elements of an effective story.	

DAY 5 ■ Writing narrative: the elements of effective fiction

Key features	Stages	Additional opportunities

Introduction

Explain that today's lesson is giving practice in writing an effective narrative in a different genre. Ask the children what they think are the features of an effective story. Tell them that there are five essential elements: Character, Setting, Plot, Conflict, Theme. List them on the board so they are displayed in the classroom and used as a prompt .

Explain that the children should make a plan before writing and that the plan will just have brief notes. Using a story planner that your children are familiar with work through the following for a story entitled 'The Missing Key'

■ Good opening – remind children that an opening can be dialogue, action or description *Use an opening which makes the reader want to read on.*

■ The ending – this helps you to write with pace and clarity. *Use a closing sentence which makes the reader think for a bit longer.*

■ Setting – think about the settings for different genres.

■ Character – it is best not to have too many in a short story.

■ First person or third person narration – encourage children to consider which best suit the story they are writing.

■ Dialogue – what characters say can help to build a picture of their thoughts and feelings.

■ Conflict or problem – there will be no tension in the story unless there is a problem. List some of the main problems that might occur.

Test practice

Time short narrative writing tasks on one of the following titles: *Lost and Found, The House on Strange Street, Robot Revolt, The Surprise Present.*

Plenary

Evaluation: give feedback to others

Children should read their work aloud. Encourage them to evaluate each other's work by providing feedback on how the stories could be improved. Reinforce the points for planning a narrative piece.

Types of question

TYPE OF QUESTION	QUESTION	ANSWER
LITERAL	What looked at Mole from a hole?	An evil wedge-shaped face looked out at him.
DEDUCE	What do you think Mole was feeling as he walked through the Wild Wood?	He was feeling frightened and he imagined that the trees were alive and threatening him.
INFER	What do you think happened after the whistling began?	I think the weasels emerged from their hiding places and attacked Mole.
EVALUATE	How effectively do you think Kenneth Grahame builds suspense in this passage?	I think Kenneth Grahame builds suspense very effectively in this passage. In particular I think he makes good use of long and short sentences to vary the pace. The short sentences, 'Then the faces began.' And 'Then the whistling began.' really create a sense of something about to happen.
JUSTIFY	Is it true to say that Mole faced his fears bravely? Use the text to answer the question.	Yes, Mole did face his fears bravely. Mole tried to convince himself that there was nothing to be afraid of. He quickened his pace and told himself not to imagine things. Even though he was scared he carried on.

The Wild Wood – test questions

1. Find one simile in the passage. Describe the effect created by that simile.

_____

_____

_____

2. Find two words that show that the faces staring out from the trees were not friendly.

_____

_____

_____

3. Find a word in the text with a similar meaning to 'faster'.

_____

_____

_____

4. What time of day is it when Mole enters the Wild Wood?

_____

_____

_____

5. Why does Mole choose to leave the path and plunge 'into the untrodden places of the wood'? Find one piece of evidence to support your idea.

_____

_____

_____

6. What do you think happens next?

_____

_____

_____

100 LITERACY FRAMEWORK LESSONS YEAR 6

PHOTOCOPIABLE   ■SCHOLASTIC
www.scholastic.co.uk

Lady Naga – test questions

◼ Answer the questions, continuing on a separate sheet of paper if you need to.

1. What does the author describe as 'magnificent'?

_____

2. What do you think a wind-rider is in *'A few wind-riders were hanging on the thermals overhead....'*?

_____

3. Why do you think the servant girl ignored Theo?

_____

4. What is the name of the gorge?

_____

5. What did Theo think was the reason for Lady Naga's visit?

_____

6. Why did Theo join the Green Storm?

_____

7. What is a balustrade?

_____

8. What is wrong with the balustrade?

_____

9. What sort of person do you think Theo is? Give evidence from the text.

_____

10. Describe the view of the gorge in your own words.

_____

Battle of Britain – test questions

■ Answer the questions, continuing on a separate sheet of paper if you need to.

1. What did the pilot decide to do after he got hit?

    _____

2. Whose was the voice?

    _____

3. What do you think was the R/T?

    _____

4. Why is the parachute being described as a mushroom?

    _____

5. How does the author describe the plane crashing?

    _____

6. Why does the narrator describe himself as a puppet?

    _____

7. What was going to 'blow'?

    _____

8. What sort of person do you think the narrator is? (Use examples from the text to help explain your answer.)

    _____

9. What do you think it means by 'teeth-clenching pain'?

    _____

10. When do you think the story was set?

    _____

■ 100 LITERACY FRAMEWORK LESSONS YEAR 6

PHOTOCOPIABLE   ■SCHOLASTIC
www.scholastic.co.uk

REVISION
UNIT 2 Non-fiction

This Unit is specifically designed to revisit and revise the reading and writing of non-fiction texts and the coverage of objectives in the Non-fiction section of this book. It is probably best placed in the late spring or early summer of Year 6, prior to the National Curriculum tests.

Key aspects of learning covered in this Unit

Enquiry
Children will seek the answers to their own and others' questions in their reading.

Information processing
Children will identify relevant information from a range of sources and use this as a basis for writing. They will explore and tease out the elements involved in combined and conflated text types.

Evaluation
Children will compare and evaluate the effectiveness of a wide range of non-fiction texts. They will share their own writing outcomes, discuss success criteria, give feedback to others and judge the effectiveness of their own work.

Reasoning
To fill the requirements of some text types, children will both follow and construct reasoned arguments based on available information and evidence.

Communication
Children will develop their ability to discuss effective communication in respect of both the form and the content of the non-fiction texts they are reading and writing. They will often work collaboratively in pairs and groups and will communicate outcomes orally and in writing.

Prior learning

Before starting this Unit check that the children can:
■ Recall the language and organisational features of the main non-fiction text types (recount, report, instructions, explanation, persuasion, discussion) and employ these in their writing, when appropriate.
■ Recall and employ the main features of other significant writing forms such as letters, dialogue, journalistic writing, biography and autobiography.
■ Write a variety of sentences (including compound sentences), punctuate them correctly and use them appropriately in their writing.
■ Where appropriate, organise writing into meaningful, cohesive paragraphs.
If they need further support please refer to a prior Unit or a similar Unit in Year 5.

Resources

Phase 1:
Frog Lollies by Nicola Davis ❀; *Mars* by Chris Webster ❀; *Internet dangers and delights* by Chris Webster ❀; *Stop the Rot* from www.sundownerapples.co.uk ❀; *Letter of Complaint* by Campbell Perry ❀; *Charlotte Brontë* from *Who was Chalotte Brontë?* by Kate Hubbard ❀; Photocopiable page 181 'How to write a recount'; Photocopiable page 182 'How to write a report'; Photocopiable page 183 'How to write an instruction text'; Photocopiable page 184 'How to write an explanation'; Photocopiable page 185 'How to write a persuasion text'; Photocopiable page 186 'How to write a discussion text'; Recount skeleton ❀; Non-chronological report skeleton ❀; Persuasion skeleton ❀; Discussion skeleton ❀; Instruction skeleton ❀; Explanation skeleton ❀; A selection of non-fiction texts; *Making Mountains* by Campbell Perry ❀; *From Frogspawn to Frogs Born* by Campbell Perry ❀; Photocopiable page 187 'From Frogspawn to Frogs Born – test questions'

Phase 2:
Letters written for different purposes; *Global Warming Fears* by Chris Webster ❀; *Internet dangers and delights* by Chris Webster ❀; Recount skeleton ❀; Non-chronological report skeleton ❀; Persuasion skeleton ❀; Discussion skeleton ❀; Instruction skeleton ❀; Explanation skeleton ❀

Cross-curricular opportunities

Connections can be made with topics being undertaken in other areas of the curriculum, though the focus for this Unit is on revision rather than teaching of non-fiction genres from scratch.

DAY 1 ■ Revisiting non-fiction text types

Key features	Stages	Additional opportunities

Introduction
Review with the children how to identify the different text types: Persuasion, Report, Explanation, Instruction, Recount, Discussion. Titles may give an indication of the text type as well as layout and use of language. Draw their attention to the fact that texts might be a mix of genres. For example, a procedural text such as a recipe may include an element of recount as the chef describes where they first encountered the recipe. Remind children about efficient ways of accessing the information from non-fiction texts. Show them how to access information quickly by skimming up and down the page locating headings and boxes and to get a sense of the overall structure. For more specific location of information they can scan the lines of the text to look for key words.

Information processing: identify relevant information

Independent work
Using copies of the extracts from the CD-ROM: *Frog Lollies* (explanation), *Mars* (report) and *Internet dangers and delights* (argument), *Stop the Rot* (instruction) *Letter of Complaint* (persuasion) *Charlotte Brontë* (recount) ask children, in pairs, to highlight structural and language features of each. Draw attention to both organisation and language features of each text type.

Plenary
Summarise the features and clarify the purpose of each text type in turn: explanation (how or why things work or happen); report (describing the way things are); discussion (reasoned argument); instruction (how to do something); recount (retelling events in time order); persuasion (why you should think this).
List and display the characteristics to aid revision.

DAY 2 ■ Using skeletons as visual aids to text structure

Key features	Stages	Additional opportunities

Introduction
Display a copy of text skeletons (see photocopiable pages 181 to 186) and remind the children how these can act as aide-memoire to the structure of different text types both for the reading test and for the writing test. Use one of the texts from the previous lesson, for example, *Frog lollies* to demonstrate using the Explanation skeleton from the CD-ROM, how the skeleton provides a map for this structure.

Independent work
Working with a selection of texts from a range of sources, children should use the six skeletons from the CD-ROM to demonstrate how the texts are organised.

Information processing: explore and tease out elements

Plenary
Reinforce how skeletons can be used to support children in test situations both to understand the organisation of texts in the reading comprehension papers and as a planning aid for writing.

DAY 3 ■ Annotating non-fiction texts: a closer look at reports

Key features	Stages	Additional opportunities
	### Introduction As reports may not have been studied since Year 3, use a report to demonstrate how to analyse a non-fiction text. Display the extract *Mars* from the CD-ROM. Briefly check children's understanding of the purpose of a report and indicate how the structure of this text was analysed using the skeletons in the previous lesson. Annotate and highlight the generic text structure: the introduction that orientates the reader to the subject; paragraphs dealing with different aspects of the subject. Note that these could be arranged in any order. Annotate and highlight the sentence/word level features: technical, subject specific vocabulary (*iron-oxide, solar system*); formal and impersonal language (third person – i*t is about...*); mostly present tense (*Mars is covered...*); some passive constructions (*Mars is covered with iron-oxide dust*); Conclusion (*Scientists predict...*).	**Extend:** provide more challenging texts **Support:** to help learners understand the non-chronological organisation, enlarge the text and cut into paragraphs for them to rearrange in different ways
Communication: work collaboratively in pairs	### Independent work Provide the children with copies of *Making Mountains* from the CD-ROM. In pairs ask children to analyse the text using the above techniques.	
	### Plenary Review what the children have identified in *Making Mountains*. How does this compare to the one that you worked through together? Do both extracts follow the same organisation?	

DAY 4 ■ Annotating non-fiction texts: a closer look at discussion

Key features	Stages	Additional opportunities
	### Introduction Display *Internet dangers and delights* from the CD-ROM. Briefly check children understanding of the purpose of an argument. Annotate and highlight the generic text structure: statement of the issue plus a preview of the main arguments (*dangers of chatrooms*); arguments for plus supporting evidence; arguments against plus supporting evidence; recommendation – summary and conclusion (*top tips*). Annotate and highlight the sentence/word level features: simple present tense (*an outright internet ban; shocks you into*); generic participants; logical connectives (*therefore*). Ask children to distinguish between the point of view and the reasons. For example: *Children should not wear uniform* (point of view) *because...* (reasons).	
Reasoning: construct reasoned arguments	### Speaking and listening Prepare a list of discussion topics on the board, such as *Should children wear school uniform? Dogs make better pets than cats.* and assign each topic a number. In groups of four, players take it in turns to roll a pair of dice. The player reads out the topic and then has to give two reasons to support that point of view. If the topic has already been used the player must give two reasons against.	
	### Plenary Invite groups to report on the topics. Discuss the reasons they used for and against the argument and model how to write highlighting connectives used.	

DAY 5 ▮ Hybrid texts: reading test practice

Key features	Stages	Additional opportunities

Introduction

Before the lesson choose a selection of non-fiction texts. These could be topic related. Make sure that you select texts that contain more than one text type within the text body. Look at one of the texts and ask the children to identify what text type it is. Discuss why there is more than one text type in the one text, for example the text might be a report text on habitats but there is an explanation about a specific process.

Communication:
work collaboratively in pairs
Information processing: explore elements in combined text types

Independent work

In pairs, using the selection of non-fiction texts, children should identify the text type and explain why there is more than one text type within a particular text.

Test practice

Provide copies of the extract *From Frogspawn to Frogs Born* from the CD-ROM and accompanying questions on photocopiable page 187. Implement the test under SATs conditions. Give the children a time limit.

DAY 1 ■ Letters

Key features	Stages	Additional opportunities
	Introduction Display a collection of letters written for different purposes. Ask the children if they ever write and send letters. Who do they write to? What is the purpose of them? Briefly list some of the reasons for writing letters. Acknowledge that email has in recent years replaced letter writing but letters can be kept. There are occasions when it is best to have a formal record.	**Cross-curricular:** the texts selected may be grouped thematically to relate to a topic being covered in another area of the curriculum
	Speaking and listening Use the display to initiate a discussion comparing a formal and informal letters. What similarities and differences do the children note? Draw out from the discussion: level of formality is related to the official capacity of the person to whom the letter is addressed. Compare the different forms of address and signing off. Information in letters is organised in paragraphs.	
	Independent work Set a choice of letter writing activities. For example: write a letter to a favourite relative telling them about the things you have been doing recently; write a letter to your local newspaper on an issue you feel strongly about; write a letter to a sporting association requesting information about the sport and details of how to get involved. Provide a set of prompts to aid writing.	
Communication: share outcomes orally	**Plenary** Read the letters to the rest of the class and identify the type of letter using the similarities and differences of formal and informal letters.	**Homework:** read the letters page in the local newspaper

DAY 2 ■ Compound and complex sentences

Key features	Stages	Additional opportunities
	Introduction Display *Global Warming Fears* from the CD-ROM and highlight the following section: *The earth is already experiencing unusual weather conditions...The hurricanes hit the Caribbean and Florida in 2004.* Ask the children what they notice about the section (short sentences). Explain how to change the short sentences into longer sentences. Use colons and semicolons. Point out the punctuation in the original and changed sentences: the use of the colon to indicate that what follows is the enumeration of what comes before. The semicolons separate complex items in a list.	
Communication: work collaboratively in pairs	**Speaking and listening** In pairs, ask children to create sentences starting with *although, because of, despite* and *after* and containing these pairs of words: *hippopotamus, popcorn; policeman, guitar; vampire, teddy bear.* Work through an example together: *Because his guitar was out of tune, the policeman played the banjo.* Point out how to punctuate these sentences with commas to mark subordinate clauses.	
	Independent work Give the children copies of *Global Warming Fears.* Ask the children to find examples of the semicolon used as an 'unspoken' connective.	
	Plenary Remind children that a complex sentence joins one or more dependent clauses to an independent clause. You can experiment with moving clauses to the beginning and the end of sentences to see what different effects are created.	

DAY 3 ◼ Investigating conditionals

Key features	Stages	Additional opportunities

Introduction
Display *Global Warming Fears* from the CD-ROM. Highlight the sentence: *A recent jump in greenhouse gases might be the start of faster global warming, scientists said on Monday.* What does the word *might* add to the sentence? Discuss the difference in meaning if the word *might* is replaced with *will*. This sentence is speculating about the possible effect of increased greenhouse gases. Explain that this is a conditional sentence in which one thing depends upon another. In this case: If greenhouse gases increase then global warming might speed up.

Display *Internet dangers and delights* from the CD-ROM. Highlight the sentence: *If your child changes what is on the computer screen when you walk in the room, or stays up late into the night surfing the internet, how do you know what sites they are visiting or who is 'visiting' them?* Explain that this sentence is saying *if* this happens, *then* how do you know that happens. Note that conditional sentences often contain the conjunction *if.*

Communication: work collaboratively in groups

Independent work
Oral practice: In a circle play the *if* game. Ask children to create sentences using the *if...then* model, for example: *If I had a magic wand then I would...*

Plenary
Play with exaggerated sentences using the model *Unless...I will not/may not be able to...* for example: *Unless I win the lottery...*

DAY 4 ◼ Connectives for different text types

Key features	Stages	Additional opportunities

Introduction
Using a selection of non-fiction texts that have been used in previous lessons, ask children to work in pairs or small groups to highlight and classify examples of connectives in different text types. Different groups can work on different text types.

Independent work

Discussion	Instruction	Persuasion	Explanation	Report	Recount
However	Mix First				

Gather the class together and write the above grid on the board. Complete the grid using the connectives that each group has found. Extend as necessary.

Plenary
Work through the examples from the grid reinforcing the types of connectives used in different text types and clarifying as necessary. Remind the children that they should use an appropriate range of connectives in their written tasks to secure good marks.

DAY 5 ■ Playing with Paragraphs: using the skeletons to structure paragraphs

Key features	Stages	Additional opportunities
	Introduction Display the Report skeleton from the CD-ROM. Choose a topic to write about from a current project being studied, such as a history topic. Fill in the skeleton with information that the children give you. Start with the title (discussing the various differences of titles for each text type) and then fill in the other parts of the skeleton. Once the skeleton is complete write a report using the information. Focus on how to structure paragraphs by using each circle of the skeleton as the information for different paragraphs. Discuss an opening paragraph and then follow the report skeleton. Highlight any topic words that might need examples and highlight any connectives or refer to the grid made in Day 4 for examples of appropriate connectives. **Test questions** Time a short non-fiction writing tasks based on a current topic, for example an explanation about a science process, a report on an historic topic or a discussion about an environmental issue. Print off the skeletons from the CD-ROM and copy them so that the children can choose which skeleton is appropriate for their text type. Ask the children to use the skeleton to help structure their writing but time this part of the test so that the children know when to begin writing the actual text.	**Cross-curricular:** the texts used for this Phase may relate to work being undertaken in other curriculum areas

How to write a recount

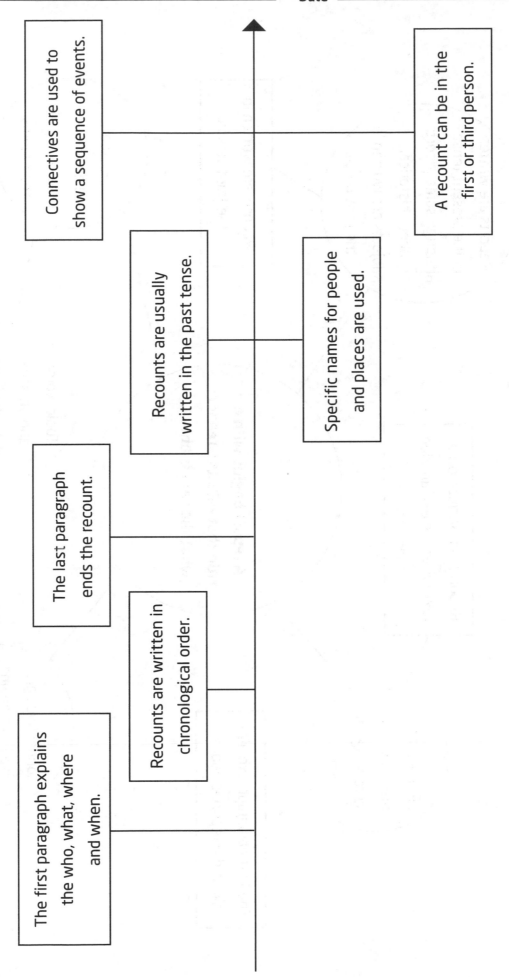

Connectives are used to show a sequence of events.

A recount can be in the first or third person.

Recounts are usually written in the past tense.

Specific names for people and places are used.

The last paragraph ends the recount.

Recounts are written in chronological order.

The first paragraph explains the who, what, where and when.

How to write a report

A report begins with a title that tells the reader what the text is about.

Reports are written in the present tense although some reports about historical subjects are written in the past tense.

Reports are written in the third person.

Factual adjectives are used to explain topic words.

Topic words and phrases are sometimes followed by examples.

Reports may include other text types like explanation or instruction.

Connectives are used to explain and contrast words.

Reports are written in non-chronological order.

The first paragraph explains what the report is about.

How to write an instruction text

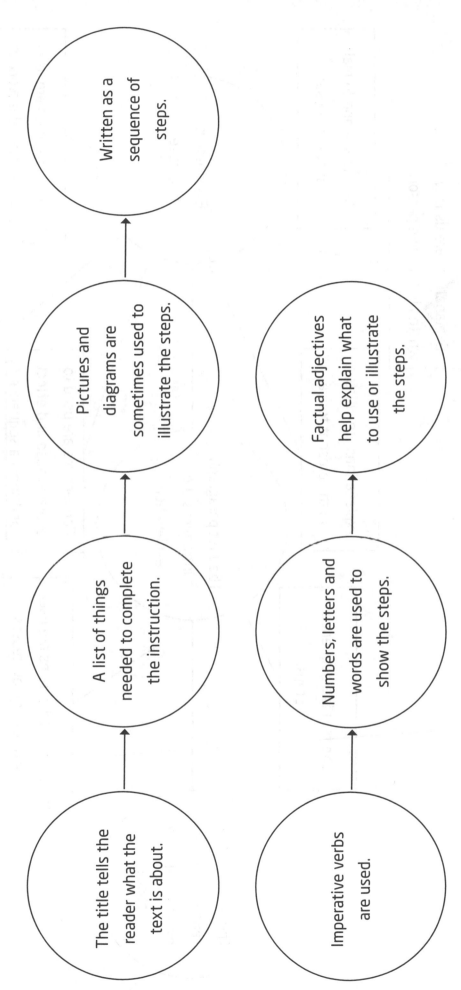

A diagram of connected circles:

- Written as a sequence of steps.
- Pictures and diagrams are sometimes used to illustrate the steps.
- A list of things needed to complete the instruction.
- The title tells the reader what the text is about.
- Factual adjectives help explain what to use or illustrate the steps.
- Numbers, letters and words are used to show the steps.
- Imperative verbs are used.

How to write an explanation

Name

Date

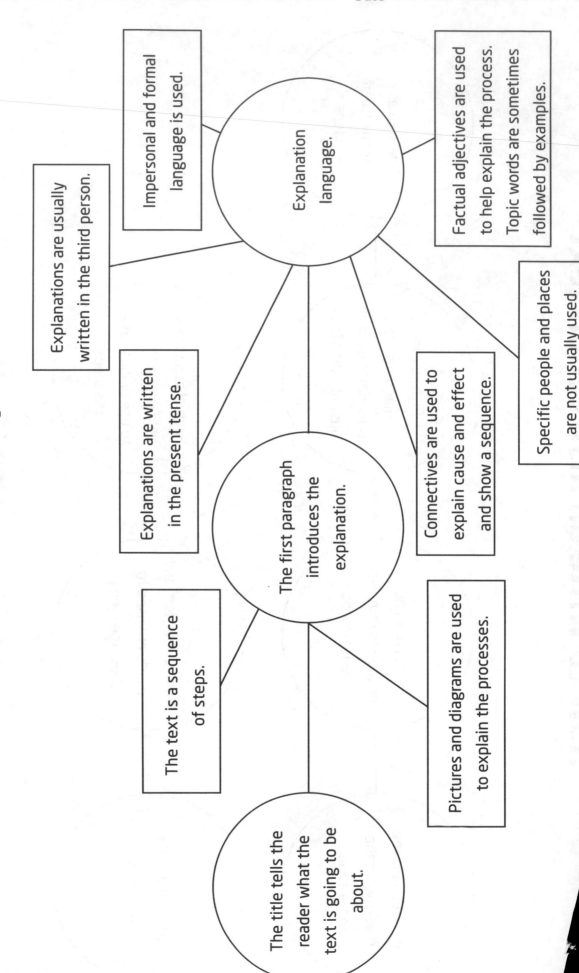

Explanation language.

Impersonal and formal language is used.

Explanations are usually written in the third person.

Factual adjectives are used to help explain the process. Topic words are sometimes followed by examples.

Specific people and places are not usually used.

Explanations are written in the present tense.

The first paragraph introduces the explanation.

Connectives are used to explain cause and effect and show a sequence.

The text is a sequence of steps.

Pictures and diagrams are used to explain the processes.

The title tells the reader what the text is going to be about.

How to write a persuasive text

REVISION ■ UNIT 2

1.

| The first paragraph introduces the point being argued. |

| A persuasive text can be in the first, second or third person as it depends on whether it is formal or informal. |

2.

| Each paragraph should explain one reason in order to persuade the reader to agree with the argument. |

| Powerful words are used to help exaggerate a point being made. |

| Connectives are used to indicate cause and effect. |

| Final paragraph repeats all the reasons of the argument. |

| Connectives are used to move from one point to the next. |

Name _____   Date _____

How to write a discussion text

The title is usually a question.	First paragraph explains what the discussion/argument is.

 Each paragraph explains one point about the argument from the opposing sides with supporting evidence.

Point 1

 A discussion text is written in the present tense. General nouns are used as well as logical connectives The points of the argument move from the general to the specific. Sometimes emotive language is used to try and persuade the reader to choose one side or the other.

Point 2

Point 3

* The last paragraph is a summary of the argument.

From Frogspawn to Frogs Born - test questions

■ Answer the questions, continuing on a separate sheet of paper if you need to.

1. What is the purpose of the first paragraph?

_____

2. What is frogspawn?

_____

3. What does a tadpole look like?

_____

4. What does a tadpole grow first?

_____

5. What text type is this? Report? Explanation? Both?

_____

6. What text type is the fact box?

_____

7. What does it mean to be 'cold blooded'?

_____

8. Can you identify any factual descriptive words?

_____

9. Are there any words which are helping to show a sequence?

_____

0. Why do you think the author chose the title *From Frogspawn to Frogs Born*?

_____

Why are there numbers in the text?

_____

REVISION
UNIT 3 Poetry

This Unit is specifically designed to revisit and revise the reading and writing of fiction and the coverage of objectives in the Poetry section of this book. It is probably best placed in the late spring or early summer of Year 6, prior to the National Curriculum tests.

Key aspects of learning covered in this Unit:

Enquiry
Children will seek the answers to their own and others' questions in their reading.

Information processing
Children will identify relevant information from a range of sources and use this as a basis for writing. They will explore and tease out the elements involved in combined and conflated text types.

Evaluation
Children will review their own answers and writing outcomes, as well as those of others. They will discuss success criteria, give feedback to others and judge the effectiveness of their own work.

Reasoning
To fill the requirements of some questions, children will construct reasoned arguments based on available information and evidence.

Self-awareness
Children will discuss and reflect on their personal responses to texts.

Communication
Children will develop their ability to discuss effective communication in respect of both the form and the content of poetry texts they are reading. They will sometimes work collaboratively in pairs and groups. They will communicate outcomes orally and in writing.

Prior learning

Before starting this Unit check that the children can:
■ Discuss responses to a range of poetry they have read.
■ Identify and discuss features of a poem, including the structure and organisation of the text and the way language is used to create effects.
If they need further support please refer to a prior Unit or a similar Unit in Year 5.

Resources

Phase 1:
Jersey Lizard by Celia Warren ❀; *Mum* by Andrew Fusek Peters and Polly Peters ❀; *From the Pied Piper of Hamelin* by Robert Browning ❀; *Haikus* by John Foster ❀; Presentation software (optional); *From a Railway Carriage* by Robert Louis Stephenson ❀; Photocopiable page 192 'From a Railway Carriage – test questions'

Cross-curricular opportunities

In addition to the poems selected for revision, supplementary poems may also be used that link other curriculum topics being studied at the time of teaching this Unit.

▶

DAY 1 ■ Revising alliteration and assonance

Key features	Stages	Additional opportunities
Self-awareness: discuss personal responses to the text	**Introduction** Display *Jersey Lizard* from the CD-ROM. Read it aloud expressively. Invite first responses: *What did you like about this poem?*	**Vocabulary extension:** create a list of words to describe the lizard's appearance
Enquiry: generate answers to questions	**Speaking and listening** In pairs, ask the children to discuss the images of the jewels and the lizard that are created in the poem. Draw out the contrast between the lizard's appearance, and its stillness, and jewels in glass cases. Consider what is similar about the jewels and the lizard (its setting acting as a foil to its appearance) as well as the human behaviour and the lizard's (finding sanctuary from the heat). Model an analysis of the poem, highlighting key features and annotating. For example, ask the children to find an example of alliteration. Ask children to consider why Celia Warren might have chosen to combine alliteration with use of a series of diverse short vowels *vibrato chest with rapid pulse, in brief relief from hostile heat.* Encourage the children to think about the speed of a lizard's heartbeat and how this is conveyed by the onomatopoeic staccato effect of the short vowels. Consider the contrasting effect of the alliteration and use of long vowel sounds in the opening and closing stanzas – the continuous sound is more drawn out and accentuates the coolness and stillness of the room. Notice how many vowel sounds in the first two stanzas are repeated in word-pairs: *cool room/stones cold/precious settings/crystal pigs.* What effect does this create? How does it help the reader to notice and observe each separate item as if they were walking into the room?	**Vocabulary extension:** sidled nursery
	Independent work Encourage the children to work with a partner to practise tongue twisters such as *Peter Piper picked a peck of pickled pepper.* Ask the children to create their own tongue twisters for each consonant letter of the alphabet, for example *Bees and bugs buzz busily beside the bus.* Who can make the most difficult alliterative tongue twister?	
	Plenary Remind the children that they should be able to talk about the effect of the poet's language choices as well as identify the devices used. Re-read the poem and reinforce the term *alliteration.* Remind the children that poets sometimes use other patterns of sound such as assonance and onomatopoeia. Ask for examples and write them on the board.	

DAY 2 ◼ Revising similes and metaphors

Key features	Stages	Additional opportunities
Enquiry: generate answers to questions **Communication:** communicate outcomes orally	**Introduction** In pairs, ask the children to read *Jersey Lizard* aloud. Remind children that when they have studied poems in the past they have seen how poets also use visual imagery to create interesting ways of looking at the world. **Speaking and listening** Revise the term *simile*. Highlight the line *like cakes in a baker's window*. How does this image compare to the jewels protected in a glass case? Highlight the phrase *A gem set in sumptuous royal blue*. What does this mean? How effectively does this describe the way the small lizard looked against the deep blue carpet? Consider how verb choice can help create a very precise image. For example: *What words might have been used instead of scurry (such as race, rush)? Is scurry better than the other possibilities? What is special about the way Celia Warren has used language here?* She uses the verb like a noun, a scurry, so that it becomes a metaphor for the lizard, imitating how the observer saw the movement before knowing *what* was moving. Revise the term *metaphor*. Ask the children to identify another metaphor describing the lizard (*a breathing rock*). **Independent work** Write a short evaluation of *Jersey Lizard* explaining how Celia Warren uses both patterns of sound (alliteration and assonance) and visual images (metaphor and simile) to create an image of the lizard. **Plenary** Review the use of sound patterns and visual imagery.	**Vocabulary extension:** flared neon **Vocabulary extension:** shawl **Support:** work on similes and metaphors

DAY 3 ◼ Kennings and riddles

Key features	Stages	Additional opportunities
Self-awareness: discuss personal responses to the text	**Introduction** Ask the children if they know any riddles. Give some quick examples such as *What gets wet when drying?* (A towel.) Display and read the poem *Mum* from the CD-ROM (blank out the title, first line and last line). Ask the children what they think the poem is about and what patterns do they notice. Point out that each line in the list is a figurative compound expression. Explain that this type of expression is called a kenning and it's a kind of riddle. Remind the children that kennings were an Anglo Saxon literary device. **Speaking and listening** Check that children understand the words *dispenser* and *constant*. Use dictionaries to check meaning and clarify in the context of the poem. In pairs, ask children to generate a list of kennings to describe a favourite sports personality, friend or celebrity. **Independent work** Write a kenning poem entitled Dad and starting *He's a...* (or about any relative friend of a favourite personality.) **Plenary** Review what has been learned about riddles. Add examples to a poetry wall (a display of illustrative examples of different forms of poetry.)	**Punctuation:** use of the colon **Punctuation:** us of hyphen; use of exclamation mark and parentheses **Support:** make kenning labels objects in the classroom (fo example a wi might be *wc viewer*)

DAY 4 ◾ Narrative Poems

Key features	Stages	Additional opportunities
	### Introduction Revise the term *Narrative poem*. Display *From the Pied Piper of Hamelin* from the CD-ROM. Tell the story of the *Pied Piper of Hamelin* up to the point where the extract starts: Hamelin was a town overrun with rats. The council in desperation offered to pay a piper a large sum of money to rid the city of the plague.	**Support:** Find examples of narrative poems in classroom collections and anthologies; read favourites in small groups and prepare to present them to the class
Enquiry: seek the answers to their own and others' questions in their reading	### Speaking and listening With the class or in small groups, hot-seat the Piper and ask questions: *Where did he come from? What are his intentions? Where did he learn to pay the pipe so skilfully? Why does he travel from place to place?* Continue the story explaining that the mayor refuses to pay the agreed sum offering only 50 guilders instead of the agreed 50,000. In pairs, ask the children to predict what might happen next.	
	### Independent work In small groups, discuss the poetic techniques that Robert Browning uses to create this scene. Highlight and annotate the text.	
	### Plenary Ask the children to think about the effects of the language. Guide and challenge them to consider the use of repetition, the variation in rhyme scheme, listing, use of high proportion of monosyllabic words in the list.	

DAY 5 ◾ Haiku and syllables

Key features	Stages	Additional opportunities
	### Introduction Display the two haiku poems from the CD-ROM . Ask the children what they notice about the two poems (each three lines, 7 – 5 – 7 syllabic structure). If necessary, remind the children that haiku is a syllabic form of poetry. Based on the Japanese tradition, haiku is a short, three line poem with 17 syllables (5. 7, 5). Model writing a haiku, demonstrating how to count syllables. Explain that haiku are intended us to think about the natural world in a new way.	**Support:** provide a simple explanation of a syllable; play a simple clapping game for a train; one clap for each syllable to imitate the rhythm of a train
	### Independent work Invite children to write their own haiku about an object or the natural world for example raindrop, puddle, snowflake. These can be presented as multimedia poems using presentation software. Use images, recorded sound and the words of the children's haiku poems in the presentations.	
	### Test Provide the children with copies of *From a Railway Carriage* from the CD-ROM and the questions on photocopiable page 192. Set a time limit.	

From a Railway Carriage –
test questions

■ Answer the questions, continuing on a separate sheet of paper if you need to.

1. What do you like/dislike about the poem?

_____

2. Can you identify any alliteration?

_____

3. How does the rhyme affect the poem?

_____

4. Is the pace of the poem fast or slow? (Please explain your answer.)

_____

5. What is 'faster than fairies, faster than witches'?

_____

6. What words or phrases show that this was written in the past?

_____

7. Can you identify any similes?

_____

8. What is being compared to 'troops in the battle'?

_____

9. Why did the poet choose that phrase 'troops in a battle'?

_____

10. Are the 'sights' actually gone forever?

_____

PHOTOCOPIABLE ■ S.C
www.